French Country

JUNK
CHIC

French Country
JUNK CHIC

KATHRYN ELLIOTT

Sterling Publishing Co., Inc. New York
A Sterling / Chapelle Book

ACKNOWLEDGMENTS

*Thank you to Jo Packham and
her staff at Chapelle for
cheering me on through round two.*

*To Diane Leis, our gifted photographer,
who captured the spirit
of our home so beautifully.*

*To Cathy Sexton, my miracle-worker editor,
who is a new lifelong friend
and an angel in disguise.*

*To my family,
who are all on to me and love me anyway.*

Library of Congress Cataloging-in-Publication Data

Elliott, Kathryn.
    French country : junk chic / Kathryn Elliott.
        p. cm.
    ISBN 1-4027-0244-2
    1. House furnishings. 2. Interior decoration.
    3. Decoration and ornament, Rustic--France. I. Title.
TX311 .E45 2003
747--dc21
                       2002152114

Published by Sterling Publishing Co., Inc.
387 Park Avenue South, New York, NY 10016
© 2003 by Kathryn Elliott
Distributed in Canada by Sterling Publishing
c/o Canadian Manda Group, One Atlantic Avenue, Suite 105
Toronto, Ontario, Canada M6K 3E7
Distributed in Great Britain by Chrysalis Books
64 Brewery Road, London N7 9NT, England
Distributed in Australia by Capricorn Link (Australia) Pty. Ltd.
P.O. Box 704, Windsor, NSW 2756, Australia
Printed and Bound in China
All Rights Reserved

Sterling ISBN 1-4027-0244-2

Chapelle, Ltd:
Jo Packham, Sara Toliver, Cindy Stoeckl
Cathy Sexton, Editor
Caroll Shreeve, Editorial Director
Karla Haberstich, Art Director
Kim Taylor, Graphic Illustrator
Marilyn Goff, Copy Editor
Diane Leis, Photographer
*Staff: Areta Bingham, Ray Cornia, Susan
Jorgensen, Emily Kirk, Barbara Milburn,
Karmen Quinney, Desirée Wybrow*

If you have any questions or comments or would like information on specialty products featured in this book, please contact:

Chapelle, Ltd., Inc.
P.O. Box 9252, Ogden, UT 84409
(801) 621-2777 • (801) 621-2788 Fax
e-mail: chapelle@chapelleltd.com
web site: www.chapelleltd.com

ABOUT THE
AUTHOR

Me playing dress-up.

*Me catching my breath
after a successful day
at the thrift store.*

Kathryn Elliott has worked as a design consultant for over 20 years. She is an accomplished artist and has sold her works successfully through galleries in Palm Springs and Malibu, California. She works as a freelance decorative paint artist and muralist, as well as an instructor on faux and decorative paint techniques.

Elliott's first published work, *Junk Chic*, is a best-seller. As a result of her book's success, she is currently appearing on a monthly decorating segment for a local ABC affiliate talk show.

Elliott has been married to her soul mate for 24 years and together they enjoy six children. They currently reside in West Linn, Oregon.

*This book is dedicated
to my one and only
true treasure—my family.
They are what makes
my home,
Heaven-on-Earth!*

CONTENTS

From Junk to Objets d'Art 8

The Search Begins 10

The Day's Findings Must Be Stored 12

Before You Begin 13

Welcome To Our Oregon Home 14

Before, During & After 16

Kitchen & Bistro 20

    Copper Cabinets 22

    Range Hood Plaques 26

    Silverware Handles & Drawer Pulls 28

    Faux-slate Wallpaper 30

    Recessed Display 33

    Countertop Displays 34

    Nutty Topiaries 36

    Cabinet-top Hutch Display 38

    Fascia Carvings 40

    Textured Soffit Tile 41

    Flower-basket Chandelier 42

    Shawl Swag Curtain 44

Formal Living Room 46

    Fireplace Hood 48

    Faux-stone Add-ons & Brackets 51

    Library Display 52

    Distressed Folding Screen 54

    Fringed Drop-cloth Drapery 58

    French Limestone Wallpaper 60

    Shower-curtain-covered Chairs 62

    Pillow Panache 65

    Headboard & Footboard Sofa 66

    Tabletop Displays 70

Dining Room & Entry 72

    Buffet Display 74

    Faux Hammered-pewter Buffet 76

    Swag-draped Wall Mirror 79

    Marbled Table 80

    Antique Mirror 83

    Cloison Display 84

    Entryway Ledge Displays 86

Master Suite 88
  Flower Rack & Bedspread Canopy 90
  Half-table Side Tables & Backdrops 92
  Lamp Shades 96
  Headboard & Mirror Wall Art 98
  Cedar-fencing Woodwork 100
  Murals 102
  Mantel Display 104
  Café Drapes 105
  Desk-top Displays 106
  Fabric & Fringe Side Chair 108
  Tiffany-style Candleholder 110
  Plant Rack Towel Shelf 112
  Side Table Luxuries 112
  Sun Stone Tile Plaques 114
  Layered Frames 115
  Framed Handmade-paper Botanical 116
  Broken-pot Relief Work 118
  Linen Layering 120
  Trading Places 120
  Vintage Candelabra 122
  Cabinet-door Sculpture 123
  Suspended Picture Frame 124
  Seashell Towel Holders 125

Guest Quarters 126
  Vintage Bed 128
  Window-frame Mirror 130
  Vintage Plate Wall Art 131
  Rose Drapery Accents 131
  Acrylic-caulk Vines 132
  Découpage Desk 134
  Black Venetian Desk Chair 136
  Framed Vintage Gloves 137
  Memo-board Collage 138
  Candlelier 139
  Wall-to-wall Frames 140
  Towel Chest 142

Le Jardin 144
  Wall Art 146
  Garden Dresser 148
  Fireplace Fountain 149
  Tray-table Pedestal 150
  Veranda Bed 152
  Topiary Screen 152
  Moss-covered Pedestal 154
Metric Conversions 155
Index 156

FROM JUNK TO OBJETS D'ART

Take your time when you walk down the bric-a-brac aisle of your local thrift store. Treasures could be hiding!

I found the brass wall ornament shown in the photo below at the thrift store. I used it as the tabletop on the "Tray-table Pedestal" on pages 150–151.

Second-hand fabrics, purchased at a fraction of the cost of retail upholstery and designer varieties, will stretch your imagination and your decorating dollars.

Fabric of any kind in any form—be it linens, clothing, or remnants—is fair game for decorating. Some of my favorite dress-ups had started out as a velvet beaded dress or a tapestry bedspread. The secret is to imagine what the item could be transformed into, then thinking it through to achieve that goal.

THE SEARCH BEGINS...

Used beds are usually plentiful at thrift stores. I've purchased all the headboard and footboard sets for my family through this source. But, after everybody had a bed, I still kept finding great bed sets that I simply had to purchase. That was my motivation to use them for other projects. See "Headboard & Footboard Sofa" on pages 66–69 and "Headboard & Mirror Wall Art" on pages 98–99.

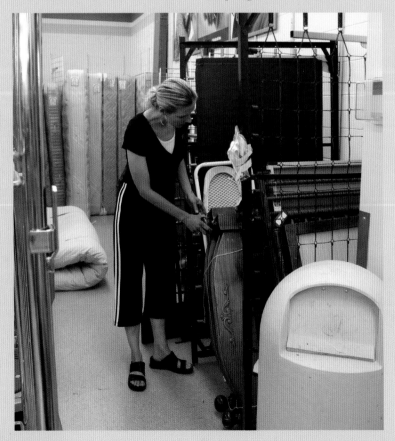

Sometimes you run across retail closeout furniture at the thrift store. The sofa table shown in the photo above is a good example of that very thing. You should not feel guilty about bringing something home that's already in great condition. The beauty of that is you can always change it in the future!

Antique trunks make for great storage and display. I have my holiday decorations hiding in trunks all over the house. Primarily I use them for displaying items of interest, but I have been known to work a little magic on them. In *Junk Chic*, I show how to turn a vintage trunk into a coffee table for a few dollars. Have you priced a reproduction trunk table?

Fabric is sold for $1.25/lb. at my favorite goodwill outlet. I have purchased all of the linens in my home there. The piece shown in the photo above would make a great sham.

The wicker chair shown in the photo at left is part of a set of three that now live on my front-yard bistro area. My friend Jo bought them for me on a junk outing we enjoyed.

...THE DAY'S FINDINGS MUST BE STORED

Even I must admit that my garage is a scary place, but everytime I go out there, it feels like Christmas. Maybe it's because I have the ability to en-vision all of my "junk" in its optimal, rein-carnated state.

You may be lucky enough to have an unused room that you can use for storing your second-hand treasures. If not, just keep in mind that the most important thing is to place your collection of junk in a dry environment.

BEFORE YOU BEGIN

Experience has taught me to always protect any exposed floors or table surfaces with adequately sized drop cloths before beginning any painting project. This simple task could save hours of clean-up and possible repair. It is imperative to work in a well-ventilated area, as many paint products have toxic fumes. Family pets and/or caged animals should never be left in these areas.

When using any product for the first time, read manufacturers' directions and recommendations. The labeling will be your best source of important information related to that product.

You can save a lot of time and money by taking paint chips to the craft store and matching colors to use in a trial application for your proposed projects. When you have determined a shade that you are happy with, an entire gallon can be mixed. For additional savings, check the mis-mixed paints at your local home center to see if there are any that would work for you.

In high-traffic areas you will want to use latex paint instead of acrylic craft paint. Latex paint will extend the life of your projects and makes cleaning easier.

A good policy to follow is: use it up, wear it out, make it do, or do without! So, always start by checking your existing resources—this also goes for project pieces. Look around your house or garage for furniture that can be recycled into a new life in a different space of your home. You will be surprised at what you already have to work with. You may be surprised that you also are a born junko-phile—absolutely addicted to collecting junk!

On a final note, be happy while you play—they say the family that "plays" together, "stays" together. And playing with junk makes it even better!

WELCOME TO OUR OREGON HOME

When we first learned we were relocating to Portland, Oregon, my first thought was how I was ever going to leave my home in Bountiful, Utah. The reluctance to leave my haven quickly turned to excitement as we began the search for a new residence. I began to think of the empty walls as blank canvas to be experimented on. When we found this contemporary-style house on Callaroga it was unique, interesting, and had great potential.

Though I have never visited France, my fascination with anything French began in junior high school when I took my first French class. I quickly realized I adored anything romantic and the very sound of the French language was the essence of romance. I was raised in a home with French and Victorian furnishings; but when I got out on my own, I went in a very contemporary direction. Through the years I have come full circle, back to the familiar look and feel of French country. The warm feeling of soft lines, scrolls, and curves tells me I'm home again.

The process of turning our newest house into an "ooh la la" of a home has been another labor of love and the end result reminds me on a daily basis that one of the greatest gifts you can give yourself is "permission to color outside the lines!"

So, come on in! Leave your preconceived notions and your feng shui fears at the front door and discover the exciting world of *Junk Chic: French Country Style*."

BEFORE...

We went from living in a *lunch pail*—our prerenovated Bountiful, Utah, home—to living in a *shoe box*—our prerenovated West Linn, Oregon, home. When we bought this home, it was the eyesore of our street and the neighbors snickered when we told them we had purchased the house. True to all my projects, the house now looks like I envisioned it the first time we pulled in the driveway. My husband and family deserve a medal for letting me drag them into all of my adventures.

Our son Braydon amidst the rubble of rock that was the beginning of the courtyard wall and fountain.

...DURING...

Yes, even those of us living in the Pacific Northwest must have sprinking systems if we want our yards to be green year-round.

. . . & AFTER

KITCHEN &
BISTRO

COPPER CABINETS

The kitchen, shown in the photo below, indicates what the cabinets looked like prior to applying the copper finish. They were contemporary, finished in a taupe-colored shiny vinyl laminate.

My biggest debate was over whether I should replace them with an eclectic mix of salvaged cupboards or simply give them a new look by using a different finish. I labored over how I would go about covering a laminate with something that wouldn't just wipe off the first time I gave the cabinets a good cleaning.

The end result is a five-step process that provides depth and contrast within the copper finish.

MATERIALS

- Cabinets
- Electric sander
- 100-grit sandpaper
- Spray paints: flat black, metallic copper
- Nylon paintbrush: 3" flat
- Flat latex paint: metallic copper
- Craft paint: metallic copper

WHAT TO DO

- Step 1: Remove doors to be refinished from cabinets, then remove all handles and hardware.
- Step 2: Using an electric sander, rough-up the surfaces of the cabinet doors. Make certain to sand in only one direction and wipe clean.

To create a cabinet finish that will imitate brushed-copper, differently colored paints are added one layer at a time. The end result will catch the light and show off the brushed strokes of copper.

STEP 4

STEP 5

STEP 6

- Step 3: Paint the surfaces of the cabinet doors with flat black spray paint. Let dry.

- Step 4: Lightly paint over the black surfaces with metallic copper spray paint, moving the can in a vertical motion. Make certain to leave some black paint showing through as this will create the bottom layer for the overall effect. Let dry.

- Step 5: Using a paintbrush, "swish" over the black/copper surfaces in a random vertical motion with metallic copper latex paint. Let dry.

- Step 6: Repeat Step 5 with metallic copper craft paint. Make certain to leave some of the previous layers of paint showing through.

- Step 7: Repeat process on cabinets, then replace handles and hardware. See "Silverware Handles & Drawer Pulls" on pages 28–29.

If cabinet doors are being permanently left off to create a lighted recessed area, the "inside" of that cabinet must be finished with the same brushed-copper layered process as the cabinets and doors. See "Recessed Display Area" on page 33.

RANGE HOOD PLAQUES

Most cabinets that are installed over a stove or cooktop that requires an overhead exhaust system aren't very practical. The cabinets are usually shallow, are positioned at a height difficult to easily access, and leave very little room for storage. I didn't have enough room in mine for anything except the salt and pepper shakers. So when this idea came about, I didn't feel like I was sacrificing anything to eliminate the cabinet.

In an ongoing effort to bring architectural interest to the galley-style kitchen, I opted to forgo the unusable space and cover it with these phenomenal plaques. The electrical outlet for the cooktop fan happened to be installed in this cupboard, so the cabinet doors could not be permanently sealed because of safety codes.

In my collection of discount-store treasures, I had this magnificent resin wall plaque.

I hung it in place across the top of the cabinet doors with construction adhesive. I didn't have anything to fit along the lower half of the vacant space, so I kept an eye out for something that would fit. It took a little while, but I couldn't have found anything more perfect than the two identical complementary pieces.

I painted all of the pieces in a verdigris color scheme that unified the three elements. The best way to duplicate a realistic look of verdigris is to find an object that is weathered in the actual finish. If the "real thing" is not available, look for a photograph in a book or magazine.

Once you have something to copy, take it to the craft store and match the finish with paint colors. I highly recommend you use a minimum of four colors of paint. Keep in mind that the more layers you apply, the more realistic the end result will be.

SILVERWARE HANDLES & DRAWER PULLS

These handles and drawer pulls add charm to cabinets that were once adorned with contemporary, chrome-plated handles. Several boxes of silver- and gold-plated flatware can be purchased for the same price as just a few handles that are manufactured to look like silverware.

This is one of those times the overall effect is benefited by a "mix and match" method. Count the number of handles and drawer pulls you will be replacing, then find mismatched silverware at a thrift store.

MATERIALS

- Electric sander
- Original handles & drawer pulls
- Mismatched silverware
- 2-part metal epoxy
- Painter's tape

WHAT TO DO

• Step 1: Using an electric sander, sand the top surfaces of the original handles and drawer pulls. Wipe clean.

• Step 2: Sand the back surfaces of the silverware. To determine which side is the "back," decide which direction the utensil will face once it is attached to the cabinet.

• Step 3: Mix the metal epoxy according to manufacturer's directions. Mix only a small amount at a time as it dries very quickly.

• Step 4: Apply a small amount of the metal epoxy to the sanded surfaces of the handles, drawer pulls, and silverware.

• Step 5: Using pressure, adhere the silverware to the handles and drawer pulls.

• Step 6: Securely wrap each silverware handle and drawer pull at the center with painter's tape. Let dry. Remove tape.

• Step 7: Replace the handles and the drawer pulls.

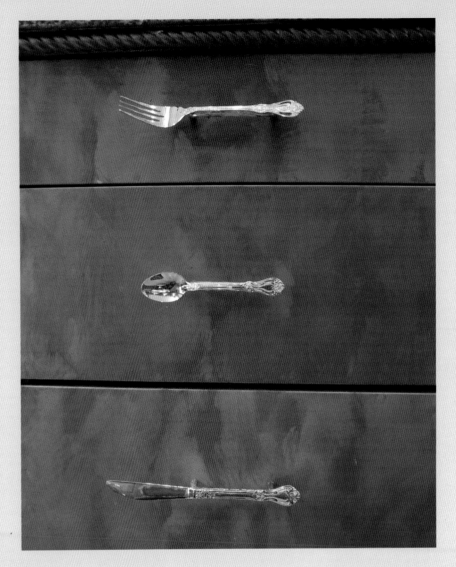

Replacing existing cabinet handles and drawer pulls can be very expensive. If you have visited the "handle aisle" at your local home center recently, you know there are literally hundreds to choose from and you also know how pricey they can be. Boxes of eight- and sixteen-piece place settings can be purchased at most dime stores, which brings your cost down to pennies. If you like an eclectic mix, as I do, any thrift store will have boxes of mismatched flatware to rummage through. Yard sales can also be a wonderful source for finding unique pieces.

FAUX-SLATE WALLPAPER

This is stock wallpaper from a local hardware store. It comes in white tones, but you can paint it any color. The secret to getting it to look like real stone is in its imperfection. This makes your job so much easier when painting it, as you don't have to worry about making it all the same.

The beautiful thing about natural stone is that there aren't any two stones that are exactly alike. By using a large sponge and three layers of color, you can achieve a realistic look without a lot of work.

MATERIALS

- Wallpaper

- Paintable acrylic latex caulk

- Synthetic sponge

- Flat latex paints: dark gray, light tan, dark taupe, off-white

WHAT TO DO

- Step 1: Hang wallpaper according to manufacturer's directions. Let dry.

- Step 2: Caulk all seams. Smooth with your finger to blend edges of wallpaper together. This will help dull the lines of the seams and make it appear less like wallpaper and more like real stone. Let dry.

- Step 3: Using a large sponge, apply the dark taupe paint over the entire surface of the wallpaper. Use a "washing" motion and allow portions of the wallpaper color to show through. Repeat with the dark gray paint.

- Step 4: Lightly apply the light tan paint over the raised surface of the stones, leaving the grout recesses dark taupe/dark gray in color.

STEP 3a

STEP 3b

- Step 5: Lightly wash over the light tan paint with the off-white paint. Make certain to leave some of the previous layers of paint showing through.

- Step 6: When all layers are painted, use the sponge to rub off some of the dark taupe/dark gray paints in the grout recesses.

STEP 4

STEP 5

RECESSED DISPLAY

See photo on page 25.

If electrical outlets are within reach, lamps can be tucked away at the back of recessed areas to enhance any mood. Depending on the amount of light desired, lamp shades can be removed and the bulb wattage can be changed.

A small table can be set in the open cabinet and used to display platters, copperware, and baskets. When choosing a table that is suitable for this application, choose one with a built-in shelf or one that has supporting cross bars.

The molding around the cabinets is stock molding from the local home center. I caulked the edges before I painted it so it would appear to have been molded into the cabinets.

33

COUNTERTOP DISPLAYS

Mirrors and small lamps may be uncommon accessories to use in a kitchen, but each creates an element of warmth and comfort. Soft lighting says "Come in, sit down, relax, and enjoy." A mirror reflects its surrounding objects and the visually pleasing aspects of the room, which only duplicates the beautiful atmosphere.

I love kitchens that don't necessarily look like kitchens, but function with all the efficiency of a gourmet playground. Therefore, I don't keep any appliances on the countertops. I would much rather look at beautiful accessories that make me want to stay and browse.

All the collectibles on the countertops are from discount stores or thrift shops. I change the configuration often so the space doesn't get visually stale. In addition, I try to find a functional use for my decorative accessories, such as using a rooster figure as a towel holder, or a small wooden box rejuvenated by beautiful tole painting to store recipes that I have clipped from my favorite magazines.

THE CHARTREUSE OF PARMA
STENDHAL
THE FRENCH CLASSICAL ROMANCES

NUTTY TOPIARIES

Have you given much thought about what to do with a partially deflated ball? These fabulous topiaries are constructed from nuts, hot glue, and thrift-store sports balls. You can use perfect balls as well, but partially inflated balls make for a better surface for glue to adhere to.

The oval topiary is a football covered with filberts and the small round topiary is a softball covered with almonds.

Basketballs covered with apples make holiday centerpieces that end up being the best conversation starters of any party.

MATERIALS

- Sports ball
- Hot-glue gun & glue sticks
- Nuts
- Container

WHAT TO DO

- Step 1: Determine which part of the ball will be the top of the topiary. Beginning at that location, hot-glue nuts in a single row in a downward direction. Repeat, adding additional rows until entire ball is covered.

If visible spaces remain and the ball underneath is not completely concealed, you can hot-glue dried moss into these areas.

- Step 2: Display topiary in a complementary container.

CABINET-TOP HUTCH DISPLAY

Shelfscaping, the art of decorating shelves, is an effective decorating technique. Here is an exaggerated example of this principle!

I had purchased this fantastic hutch at a goodwill outlet and stored it in my garage for months, waiting to find a place to use it. Because the area between the top of the cabinets and the ceiling in this kitchen is so high and the cornice is extra deep, I needed to use something to act as an elevating layer of display space. I decided that my vintage hutch would serve this purpose. My muscular sons graciously hoisted it into position for me and secured it in place.

Having this hutch as a display case is like having a little store full of wonderful things to play with. I periodically rearrange the display just for fun.

FASCIA CARVINGS

Molded plastic dresser-drawer fronts can be easily removed and applied to the cornice fascia with construction adhesive and 2" finishing nails. If decorative dresser-drawer fronts cannot be found, molded plastic or resin wall plaques are readily available and work just as well. In either case, the edges should be caulked with paintable acrylic latex caulk.

To fill in the space between each drawer front, I cut out a small square medallion from a remnant of embossed wallpaper as shown in the bottom photo at right and placed one between each drawer front as shown in the photo on page 38.

I painted the entire cornice fascia with different shades of taupes and golds to help coordinate the wall and all the add-ons.

The architectural interest these carvings provide is significant. This treatment draws your eye upward immediately upon entering the kitchen and, due to the ceiling height, makes the entire space seem larger than it really is.

TEXTURED SOFFIT TILE

The cornice soffit is finished with embossed wallpaper that I painted at the same time as the cornice fascia. I used the same shades of taupes and golds.

The embossed design adds another texture, even though the colors are the same. To eliminate your eye stopping at the seams and to unify the space, caulk all seams with paintable acrylic latex caulk.

For a more dramatic effect, try using three different coordinating colors.

If these wire-mesh hanging baskets cannot be found in the color you desire, they can be easily spray-painted with any color that coordinates with your decorating scheme. See photo on page 2.

FLOWER-BASKET CHANDELIER

At first you will probably mistake these wonderful lights for vintage amber-glass chandeliers. Now, take a closer look—they are spray-painted hanging baskets, filled with yellow and gold tissue paper.

We had discussed replacing the overhead recessed can lighting in our kitchen with a much more costly alternative, but when this "chandelier idea" was born it became the perfect solution to our lighting requirements. The concept here is using the existing lights to "light" the tissue paper inside the baskets. As a safety factor, the lengths of chain are long enough to allow plenty of air flow and disperse the heat radiating from the bulb. The recessed lights are on dimmer switches, so the output of light can be adjusted to accommodate any mood. When the lights are dimmed, the illusion of candlelight abounds.

This is my favorite thing in the whole house! In the kitchen, we went from a very harsh, unflattering light to a warm light, bathing the room in gold.

MATERIALS

- Needle-nosed pliers
- Wire-mesh hanging flower basket with three chains
- Colored tissue paper
- 3 Cup hooks

WHAT TO DO

- Step 1: Using needle-nosed pliers, remove the ring that holds the three chains together.

- Step 2: Line the inside of the flower basket with colored tissue paper.

- Step 3: At equal intervals around the outside edge of the recessed light, install the three cup hooks.

- Step 4: Hang each length of chain from each of the cup hooks.

- Step 5: Adjust the tissue paper as necessary. Once you have lighting coming through, you will be able to see where you need to add more or take some away.

SHAWL SWAG CURTAIN

I borrowed this shawl from the living room. It is folded in half over the curtain rod, then gathered on the sides with a ladder stitch. The light coming through the woven fabric is very warm and subdued. It draws your eye to the center of this window and calls attention to the table and stool grouping. The tassels are my favorite thing about this window treatment.

The drapery panels at each side of the shawl swag have been draped over the rods for a swagged effect to coordinate with the center panel. Besides, who would want to cover up the beautiful view of the green space outside?

These tassels, made from wood and fur, are casual yet elegant. Their color enhances the rich copper tones of the entire kitchen.

FORMAL LIVING ROOM

FIREPLACE HOOD

The original fireplace, shown in the photo at right, was just a flat box before we had the French fireplace hood constructed and the hearth extended with the plaster columns underneath.

Historically an authentic French hood would be used as a venting system and would be made from stone. We already had a venting system and we couldn't afford stone. The new hood was constructed using steel 2x4s and drywall. The degree of the diminishing angles had to be calculated in order to determine how far out into the room the finished fireplace would go. At first, the hood seemed overwhelming. When the columns were set and the entire surface, complete with add-ons, was papered and painted, it created an anchor for the room in addition to providing warmth and drama.

The acanthus-leaf architectural aprons were salvaged from an old building in downtown Portland. I caught up to them at my favorite local thrift store and purchased four large pieces as shown in the photo

on page 48 for $70. We had professional carpenters cut them on their diamond saw and mount them. Because the damaged areas were too big to repair and still have the faux woodwork all blend together, I opted to paint them in conjunction with the rest of the fireplace so they would appear to be molded out of the same structure.

The window in the center of the fireplace hood was placed there for a functional reason. There was a recessed can light in the middle of the hearth ceiling that I did not want to cover up. By cutting a hole in the center and hanging a wall decoration with a crocheted doily in the center, a back-lit window is simulated. At night it has a soft glow and hides the light itself, which is visible through the opening.

The four columns at the bottom aren't structural. They are plaster columns I purchased at a craft store on a buy one, get one free sale. That brought the price down to $15 each.

They are sitting on plywood boxes, then papered and painted in the same faux stonework, as shown in the photo below. See "French Limestone Wallpaper" on pages 60–61.

FAUX-STONE ADD-ONS & BRACKETS

All of the resin add-ons and wall brackets were installed with construction adhesive and caulking to give them a sculpted appearance. To achieve a natural stone finish, use the darkest layer of color of the faux stone you are blending the bracket into. The consecutive layers should be the same as the remaining colors used. The resin bird sculptures are simply sitting on top of the bracket for added impact. Add-ons can also be applied to furniture to give added stature and interest. See "Headboard & Footboard Sofa" on pages 66–69.

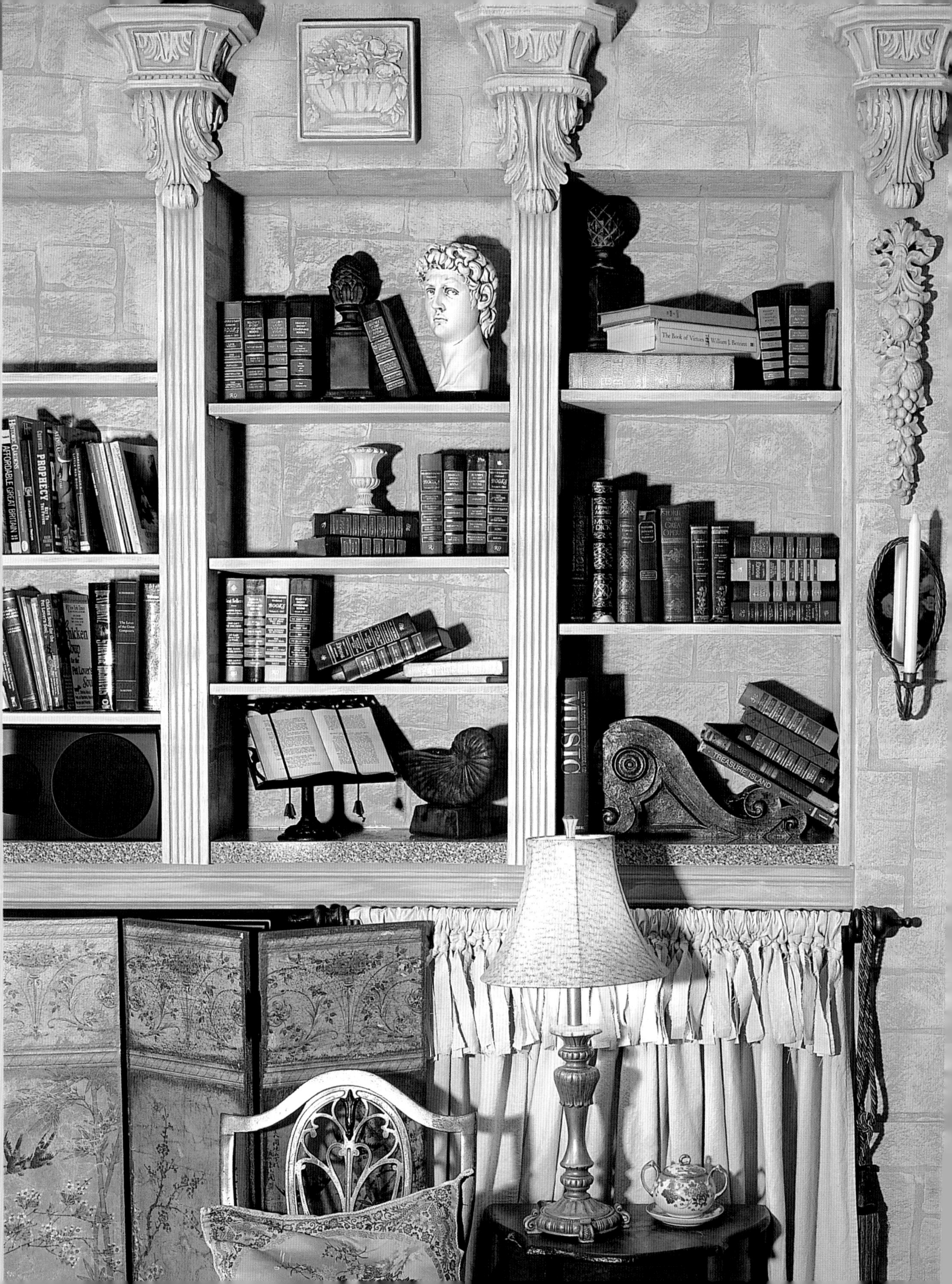

LIBRARY DISPLAY

In a wall-unit bookcase, there are many tricks which can be used to draw the eye to that part of the room.

Throughout my house, you will find books being used to create platforming for objets d'art, to elevate lamps, and to simply create a lived-in comfortable look. You can use a variety of differently sized books for the platforming technique as long as the largest book in the grouping is on the bottom of the stack. Smaller books may then be stacked in a largest to smallest format forming a base to display an object to which you want to call attention. Make certain the smallest book on the top of the stack is slightly larger than the object you are displaying to give it adequate support.

Situating books at different angles makes the books look more enticing and well read. Sometimes simply displaying a book open to a page of some particular interest can personalize a room.

A lot of my books are collected from thrift stores because they have visual character. Their covers are usually worn and slightly tattered. The literary content may not be of particular

interest to me, but because they have been read and loved by someone, they somehow look and feel like a treasured heirloom.

Large and small architectural brackets can double as bookends when placed on their sides. They also have a dramatic presence when displayed alone on a shelf. Creating a visual break from the books will make for a much more interesting display.

DISTRESSED FOLDING SCREEN

Today, a formal living room is generally the most underused room in the entire house. In fact, many homes don't even have one as they have been replaced by "family or great rooms." Many years ago, a formal living room or parlor was used as the "visiting center" in the home. Family and friends would gather to enjoy each other's company or perhaps listen to the radio. Because life nowdays is so hectic, time-out for "visiting" is sadly a thing of the past.

Our needs required that our formal living room be a space that we used. It was my challenge to figure out how to find harmony between the living room, the television, and the family. In order for this room to house the television and all of the electronic equipment, having it hidden was my prerequisite. Out of necessity, a creative solution came about. The cover-up had to be functional and child friendly, but it also had to be beautiful to fit into my decorating scheme.

The television is hidden behind this folding screen and the speakers are hidden behind the drop-cloth panels on either side.

MATERIALS

- Pressboard panels
- Table saw
- Paintbrush: 3"-wide
- Heavy-duty, water-soluble wallpaper paste
- Poster panels or other decorative paper
- Wallpaper border— vinyl cannot be used
- Synthetic sponge
- Craft paints: brown, metallic gold
- Satin acrylic spray sealer
- 2 Hinges for every side of every panel that will be connected

WHAT TO DO

- Step 1: Determine the number of pressboard panels you will need by measuring the width of the object you are trying to hide and dividing it by the width of the individual panels.

- Step 2: Using a table saw, cut each panel to the appropriate height. Most home centers will cut the wooden panels for you.

- Step 3: Measure and cut the poster panels to cover each wooden panel, allowing a little extra to fit directly up underneath the bottom edge of the border.

- Step 4: Begin distressing the poster panels by first wadding them up and getting them slightly damp under a faucet. Make certain you do not saturate the paper as it will begin to tear where it has been creased.

- Step 5: Carefully open up the poster panels and smooth them out to the best of your ability. They will have some wrinkles and tiny tears along the creases. This is the desired effect.

- Step 6: Using a paintbrush and wallpaper paste, apply the poster panels beginning at the bottom of each wooden panel. Let dry.

- Step 7: Measure and cut the wallpaper border to fit across the top of each panel.

- Step 8: Repeat Steps 4–6 to distress, smooth, and apply the lengths of wallpaper border.

- Step 9: Using a small sponge, very lightly wash over the entire panel with brown craft paint, making certain some of the paint seeps into the wrinkles on the border and paper. If you apply too much paint, dampen the sponge and wipe off excess.

- Step 10: Using the paintbrush, feather some metallic gold craft paint around all of the outside edges of each panel. Blend the metallic gold paint along the inside edge into a blurred line between the metallic gold border and the panel itself.

- Step 11: Using the sponge, lightly wash some metallic gold craft paint over

the top of the wrinkles, in randomly selected areas of each panel. Let dry.

- Step 12: Seal each of the panels with satin acrylic spray sealer. Let dry.

- Step 13: Using two hinges between each connecting panel, assemble the folding screen. Check to make certain screen is sturdy and can stand on its own.

FRINGED DROP-CLOTH DRAPERY

After making drapes for my formal living room out of an ordinary drop cloth, those wonderful window treatments kept popping up all over my house. They hang in many of my windows and are also used to hide the surround-sound speakers in the living room.

I folded the top of a 9' x 12' drop cloth over and hemmed it to make a rod pocket. A 6" flap of excess was left to hang below the hemmed pocket. As shown in the photo at right, this excess fabric is what is used to make the fringe. I took a measuring tape and marked off every two inches, then I cut the fabric vertically at each mark. Finally, I tied each strip into a knot. The placement of the knots can be random, but I chose to place them as close to the bottom of the rod pocket as possible.

The curtain-rod finials are resin table decorations I found at a local department store. I secured each finial to the end of a wooden closet pole, then painted them with black and gold craft paints.

I hung a tassel over the rod at the center of the drop-cloth drape, hiding the braided cord behind the fringe. A celedon-green silk panel was then hung at each side.

This unique window treatment is an inexpensive alternative to purchasing heavy ready-made drapes.

59

FRENCH LIMESTONE WALLPAPER

MATERIALS

- Wallpaper
- Paintable acrylic latex caulk
- Synthetic sponge
- Flat latex paints: light tan, dark taupe, off-white

WHAT TO DO

• Step 1: Hang wallpaper according to manufacturer's directions. Let dry.

• Step 2: Caulk all seams. Smooth with your finger to blend edges of wallpaper together. This will help dull the lines of the seams and make it appear less like wallpaper and more like real stone. Let dry.

• Step 3: Using a large sponge, apply the dark taupe paint over the entire surface of the wallpaper. Use a "washing" motion and allow portions of the wallpaper color to show through.

• Step 4: Lightly apply the light tan paint over the raised surface of the stones, leaving the grout recesses dark taupe in color.

• Step 5: Lightly wash over the light tan paint with the off-white paint. Make certain to leave some of the previous layers of paint showing through.

STEP 3

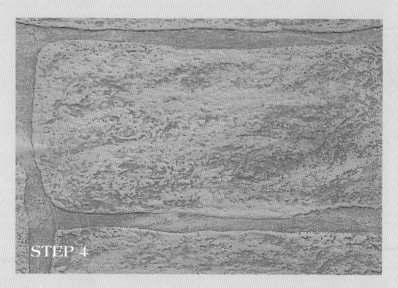

STEP 4

STEP 5

SHOWER-CURTAIN-COVERED CHAIRS

I have been reupholstering furniture with this hot-glue-gun technique for years, and I still get excited with the results everytime I re-cover a piece of furniture. Because the process is so simple, I have been known to change the upholstery on the same piece of furniture time and again. Such is the case with these chairs.

I had originally covered them with red velvet and the result was so dramatic, no one would have ever guessed that I had rescued these chairs from the curb on trash-pickup day.

MATERIALS

- Upholstered chairs
- Damask fabric shower curtain
- Hot-glue gun & glue sticks
- Scissors or craft knife
- Chenille yarn
- Transparent tape

WHAT TO DO

- Step 1: Measure all areas of the chair that are currently uphol-stered. Add an addi-tional 3" on all edges to allow for pulling and gluing.

- Step 2: Cut a piece of fabric and drape it over the chair seat so the seat is completely covered. Begin cover-ing the chair seat by applying hot glue to the front-bottom edge of the chair. Apply the edge of the fabric to the glue. Once the front edge has fused, pull the fabric and hot-glue the back-bottom edge in place. Glue any excess fabric under the seat.

- Step 3: Begin covering the front side of the chair back by applying hot glue to the top edge of the chair back. Drape the fabric to allow a 3" overhang.

After the entire front of the chair has been reuphol-stered, use scissors or a sharp craft knife to trim away all excess fabric. Make certain to trim evenly with the existing edge of the chair where the fabric on the front of the chair ends

and the fabric for the back of the chair will begin.

- Step 4: Repeat Step 3 for the back side of the chair back. The back and front edges of the newly upholstered fabric should be touching.

To alleviate wrinkling, pull the fabric taut around the edges of the chair back. After the entire back of the chair has been re-upholstered, trim all excess fabric away.

• Step 5: It is necessary to trim all of the edges to cover up the hot-glued seams. Begin on the back-bottom edge of the chair seat. Working in small sections, start applying hot glue directly along the bottom edge of the chair. Immediately apply the chenille yarn over the glue. When you need to cut the yarn, place a piece of transparent tape on it where it is to be cut. Make the cut on the opposite side of the tape. The end that will be glued down will retain the tape and help prevent it from fraying. After the hot glue is dry, the tape can be removed.

Hot-glue the yarn around all of the edges where the excess fabric has been trimmed away. This creates an instantly finished edge.

The chair shown in the photo above was one of a set of two chairs that I covered with red velvet to accent the decor in my Utah home. I added a single tassel to the back of each of the chairs with upholstery thread for added drama. These are the same chairs that I reupholstered with the damask shower curtain to complement my Oregon home.

PILLOW PANACHE

Using pillows is an important element in any decorating scheme. In my home, I choose to use pillows covered with different colors, pattern designs, and textures. The visual appeal of texture triggers the tactile senses and draws us to the object to actually touch it. This in itself helps create an environment that is comfortable and inviting. It is also important to use several differently sized pillows together to add dimension and interest.

HEADBOARD & FOOTBOARD SOFA

A $10 queen-size headboard and footboard set is transformed into this beautiful and very functional seating arrangement.

To provide enough seating for my entire family of eight, I knew one sofa would not be adequate. I like an eclectic mix of furniture styles in a room to give it personality, so I didn't want the second sofa to match the first. I found this bed set at the thrift store. It had the French look of the curved, caned back that I love and the chunky scale that I needed to balance out the oversized sofa. Luckily it was the same width as the sofa on the other side of the room, so

angling them at the same degree was easy and maintained the balance on both sides of the room.

MATERIALS

- Headboard and footboard with wooden side rails
- Pine: 1" x 6" x 8', 2 lengths
- Electric screwdriver
- Wood screws: 2"–3"
- Architectural add-on
- Construction adhesive
- Paintable acrylic latex caulk
- Paintbrush: 3"-wide
- Flat latex paints: tan, off-white
- Wallpaper cutouts
- Découpage medium
- Satin acrylic spray sealer
- 2 Decorative iron ornaments

WHAT TO DO

- Step 1: Stand the headboard and the footboard together, resting against each other.

- Step 2: Measure the height up to the bottom of the headboard rail, then measure the height to the top of the footboard. This will be where the seat will be installed, so the two height measurements must be the same. If they are not, you will need to modify either the headboard or the footboard to have compatible measurements.

- Step 3: Determine the desired depth of the seat taking into consideration the width of the decorative iron ornaments and the desired

amount of seat overhang. To make the sides, cut two pieces to that dimension from one of the lengths of pine. Using an electric screwdriver, attach each side piece between the headboard and the footboard with wood screws. Make certain to position them on the inside of the headboard and footboard posts. You should have a "box" formation when this step is complete.

• Step 4: To make the seat, use the wooden side rails. Measure the width of the headboard inside the posts and cut the side rails to that length. Measure the depth of the side rails to determine how much remaining seat depth you will need to fill in with the remaining length of pine. Eliminate the sharp corners by rounding the front of the seat.

If the wooden side rails are not available, make the entire seat from pine.

• Step 5: Using the electric screwdriver and wood screws long enough to accommodate the thickness of the seat, install the seat by screwing through the seat into the "box" until the seat, side supports, and the headboard and footboard are completely secure.

Additional seat support may need to be added at the center depending on the amount of weight the structure must support.

• Step 6: Apply the architectural add-on with construction adhesive. Let dry.

• Step 7: Caulk around all of the edges. Let dry.

• Step 8: Wipe down all wood to remove any dirt or grease. This is necessary so the paint will adhere properly. Using a paintbrush, lightly drag the tan paint over the wood, allowing portions of the raw wood to show through. Make certain your brush

strokes go in the direction of the wood grain.

• Step 9: Repeat Step 8 with off-white paint, allowing portions of the raw wood and the tan paint to show through. Let dry.

• Step 10: Apply wallpaper cutouts with découpage medium. Apply additional coats of découpage medium according to manufacturer's directions and the desired effect. Let dry.

• Step 11: Seal the entire sofa with satin acrylic spray sealer. Let dry.

• Step 12: Using the electric screwdriver and wood screws, determine the desired rail height and install one decorative iron ornament on each side for side rails.

DECORATING TIP

• Drape a tassel over one or more of the headboard or footboard posts for added interest and drama.

The side rails to this sofa are metal grates that I found at a craft store. Garden ornamentation is very easy to adapt as add-ons to furniture. I purchased these for $15 each in the finish you see here. However, if you find something wonderful that doesn't match your color scheme, you have many options for choosing an alternate finish. Metal accents are especially versatile. You can age them naturally to a rusted patina by soaking in salt water until rusted, or you can purchase "weathering" kits at your local craft store for distressing metal, bronze, copper, and brass.

TABLETOP DISPLAYS

Think of all of the tabletop surfaces you have at your decorating disposal. These are great display spaces basically just sitting around. Typically we think of wall space as the primary source of backdrop for display, but coffee tables, end tables, sofa tables, desks, mantels, and shelves can also be used to display collections of your favorite things.

On the desk, I layered tall items that would help balance the height of the room. I found this topiary at a department store for $69. They are intended for the floor, but if your ceiling is high enough, they look great elevated on a table or desk top. Eclectic items that don't necessarily have a common theme can be grouped according to size, color, or shape. Most of the objects on the desk are thrift-store collected and were chosen for their height. The lamp is painted tan over its original bright yellow finish and paired with a smaller-scale shade. Typically, a base with over-sized proportions would call for an oversized shade to balance its scale. Instead, I chose a tall shade with a narrow rim and balanced it using a vertical method rather than a horizontal one. The carved wooden shoe is actually a doorstop posing as sculpture!

Adding candles to any room radiates warmth and makes it special. Using candles has become increasingly popular. Candles themselves are becoming conversation pieces, like the coffee-scented candle I embellished by dipping it in coffee beans. Elevating a single candle on a pedestal will give it importance as will using several candles of various heights in a single grouping.

Tabletop surfaces can also be used to turn your room into a buffet for casual entertaining. A platter of breads, fruits, and cheeses, nestled among interesting and beautiful items, looks especially appealing and will blend well into any decor. To create a formal entertaining atmosphere, drop cloths can be draped over all of the tabletop surfaces to add formality and unify them visually.

DINING ROOM
& ENTRY

BUFFET DISPLAY

This dining room glows at night. The darker tones and the reflection of all the warm light in the buffet mirrors makes for a warm and inviting welcome upon entering the home.

When a dining room is the first thing you see when you open the front door, it often creates a decorating dilemma. In this instance, the room itself is narrow. The ceiling height creates the illusion of a larger space so the area doesn't seem as closed in. By adding sheet mirror to the wall behind the buffet and glass shelves, it seems as if the room continues through to another space. The dark stone wall reflected from the other side of the room keeps the overall mood of the dining room intimate, while providing extreme visual texture and backdrop for all the displayed crystal and trinkets.

All of the items collected on the glass shelves are either from discount shops or thrift stores. The common thread tying them all together is the crystal. The overhead can lights illuminate the glassware and the shelves, amplifying the entire lighting effect.

FAUX HAMMERED-PEWTER BUFFET

I wanted a built-in buffet in the formal dining room in order to tie the kitchen and dining room together. However, I didn't want to duplicate the effect of the copper in this space. I wanted the two spaces to be unified since the pass through made the two spaces visible at the same time. I was determined to carry out the metallic look in this room as well, but not overpower the room itself. I chose the faux hammered-pewter finish because it complemented the faux-rock wall.

The medallions on the fronts of the buffet doors shown in the photo on pages 74–75 are plastic wall decorations. They were all collected at different times.

MATERIALS

- Buffet
- Electric sander
- Plastic wall decorations
- Construction adhesive
- Paintable acrylic latex caulk
- Spray paints: flat black, hammered aluminum, chrome
- Nylon paintbrush: 3" flat
- Paint thinner

WHAT TO DO

- Step 1: Remove doors to be refinished from buffet, then remove all handles and hardware.

- Step 2: Using an electric sander, rough-up the surfaces of the buffet doors.

- Step 3: Apply plastic wall decorations with construction adhesive. Let dry.

- Step 4: Caulk all the edges around each add-on. Let dry.

- Step 5: Paint the surfaces of the buffet doors with flat black spray paint.

- Step 6: While the flat black spray paint is still wet, lightly paint over the black surfaces with hammered-aluminum spray paint, moving the can in a vertical motion. Make certain to leave some black paint showing through as this will create the bottom layer for the over-all effect. The hammered-aluminum spray paint should start to "bubble" revealing the black undercoat in spots.

• Step 7: Using a paintbrush, "flick" paint thinner onto the black/aluminum surfaces. Small amounts of paint thinner should "pool" into drops.

• Step 8: While the paint thinner is still pooled, lightly paint over the black/aluminum surfaces with chrome spray paint, moving the can in a vertical motion. Make certain to leave some of the previous layers showing through.

• Step 9: Repeat Steps 2–8 on the buffet doors. The re-petitive layers of paint will determine the translucent end result of the faux ham-mered-pewter effect.

• Step 10: Repeat process on cabinets, then replace the hardware.

STEP 6

STEP 7

STEP 8

The ornamental iron grates suspended over the buffet were $14.99 each and I hung them with cup hooks. I washed the gold finish with a sponge and brown craft paint to age the appearance. The beauty of hanging them in front of a mirror is that you double the drama!

SWAG-DRAPED WALL MIRROR

Draperies aren't just for windows anymore! They can be hung wherever you want to add a little drama, break up a long wall, or to call attention to something of special interest. Here the drapery scarf accentuates the large mirror that hangs on the wall above the patio doors. I love the reflection of the flower-basket chandeliers that hang over the dining-room table.

MARBLED TABLE

This table already had the latticed inlayed pattern that I used as a guide for this design. After the entire table was painted black, the sections between the inlayed patterns were layered with all the colors found in natural slate—grey, gold, rust, brown, and black. I then took a kitchen paring knife and literally scratched off the paint in a marble-veining pattern. Vinegar was splashed onto and wiped over the entire table surface, dragging off some of the paint.

The center section of the table with faux-marble inlay was created using manufactured black-and-white contact paper. A wash of brown craft paint was applied over the contact paper with a sponge. Once dry, some of it was wiped off allowing portions of the contact paper to show through. To simulate marble veining, I used a streaking pattern to remove some of the brown paint.

I made an argyle template and traced it around the table edge, filling in with metallic silver and metallic gold paints as shown in the photo on page 82. I gold-leafed the raised elements on the legs and sanded off some black areas, exposing the rosy tone underneath. Seven coats of acrylic polyurethane sealer now protect the surface.

The two table sections meet pattern to pattern, even though the colors are contrasting. When placed together they simulate an inlay effect. The amber-colored veining was hand-painted.

ANTIQUE MIRROR

Having a mirror resilvered is very expensive and, depending on where you live, it is often-times difficult to find a glass company that offers this service. Learn to enjoy the authenticity of aged mirrors, or create your own!

There is no need to search high and low for an expensive antique mirror complete with distressed glass. You can create the illusion of age by distressing the back of the mirror itself.

By spattering some paint thinner on the silver paint on the back of the mirror and lightly sanding off the softened paint, you can gently remove the paint and add years to your mirror. You will want to make certain the sandpaper you are using is extra-fine. A light spattering of brown or black craft paint on the front side of the mirror adds to the faux aging as well. To further the illusion, back the mirror with brown packing paper or black butcher paper. This will tone the missing sections of paint and give the mirror a finished look.

CLOISON DISPLAY

The top of the room partition dividing the formal living room and the dining room, known as the cloison, is a wonderful unexpected area for display. The fascia is adorned with resin- and plaster-formed ornamentation that I permanently installed using construction adhesive and paintable acrylic latex caulk, carefully blended into the faux-stone surfaces. This process makes them appear as if they were actually carved out of the stone. The final step is to paint the add-ons in the same color scheme, using the same painting techniques, as the faux-stone walls. When done successfully, your eye will travel seamlessly over everything you have added.

The display itself is comprised of uncommon objects sharing a common space. Paintings stand out when they are displayed in unusual ways. Propping one against another object large enough to support it is a good substitute for a lack of available wall space.

Large pots and/or baskets that would normally be difficult to fit into limited floor space can live happily together on cloison tops. The added benefits are plentiful when you consider all the additional "toys" you can show off.

ENTRYWAY
LEDGE DISPLAYS

Our entryway is small, but features a 12' ceiling that exaggerates the size. The built-in ledges overhead give visual interest and draw your eye upward. Instead of being a small, boring entry, a welcoming and intriguing entrance to the home is created.

On one side of the entry, the recessed ledge is the home for stacked luggage, a painting, and baskets, which are all from thrift stores. Make certain you take advantage of the extra storage space. I use my vintage luggage to store Christmas ornaments that are especially delicate.

On the opposite side, a coffee table sits atop the

recessed area and is adorned with baskets and pots to make the space

seem a little more casual. I purchased the coffee table at the goodwill outlet for $5.

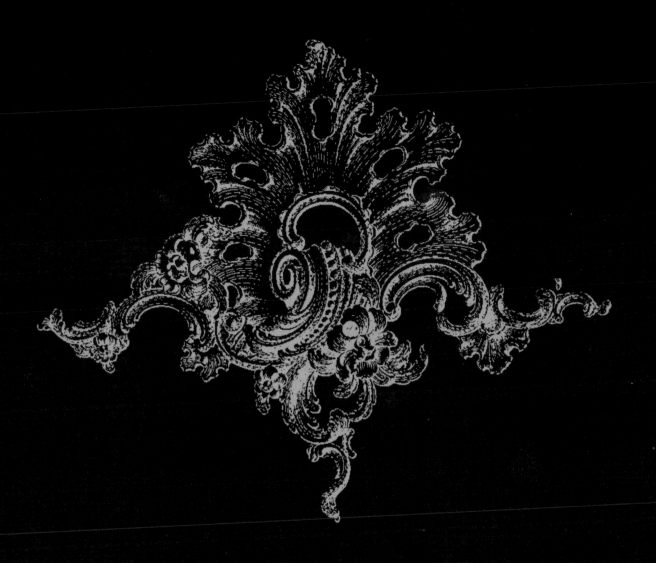

MASTER
SUITE

FLOWER RACK & BEDSPREAD CANOPY

Our master bedroom is the result of creative ideas derived from intense problem-solving sessions. I adore this room because it reminds me daily that our creativity is limited only by the conforming factors we allow ourselves to be concerned with.

MATERIALS

- Flower rack
- Electric drill & drill bits
- Drywall anchors
- Scissors
- Bedspread
- Curtain hooks

WHAT TO DO

- Step 1: Because the canopy must be centered above the bed, determine the center of the bed and mark the wall accordingly at the height you will be hanging the flower rack.

- Step 2: Using an electric drill, install the flower rack with drywall anchors.

- Step 3: Cut the bedspread in half lengthwise. Push the curtain hooks through the top edges of both pieces of bedspread.

- Step 4: Spacing evenly, attach the hooks to the flower rack.

- Step 5: Tie back or drape panels to the sides.

Visually this wall has a lot going on and I wanted to use a tassel that wouldn't be overwhelming for the space. These glass pears, attached to a length of chenille yarn, were perfect.

91

HALF-TABLE
SIDE TABLES
& BACKDROPS

These fabulous side tables and backdrops give the illusion of built-ins around the bed.

The side tables are the result of literally cutting a dining table in half and using one half on each side of the bed. The backdrops are 36" hollow-core doors purchased for $18 each at the local hardware store. The partitions were created with inexpensive pine framing materials.

The backdrops were embellished with strips of wallpaper border, molded resin wall plaques, and mirrored tile.

MATERIALS

- 2 Hollow-core doors without predrilled holes for doorknobs, 36"-wide

- Dining table, 36" wide

- Wallpaper borders: embossed, flat

- Relief plaques

- 2 Mirrored tiles

- 1" x 2" Pine lattice strips

- Handsaw

- Construction adhesive

- Sponge

- Craft paint, metallic gold

- Paintbrush, wide

- Heavy-duty wallpaper paste

- Mirror adhesive

- Paintable acrylic latex caulk

- Flat latex paints: gold, taupe

- Electric screwdriver

- Wood screws

- Skillsaw

- 2 Decorative sconces

WHAT TO DO

- Step 1: Lay each door on a flat surface with plenty of maneuvering room on all sides.

- Step 2: First, determine the height of the side tables. Then determine the layout of the wallpaper borders, relief plaques, and mirrored tiles on each door, making certain all decorative work is to be done above the side tables. The layout of

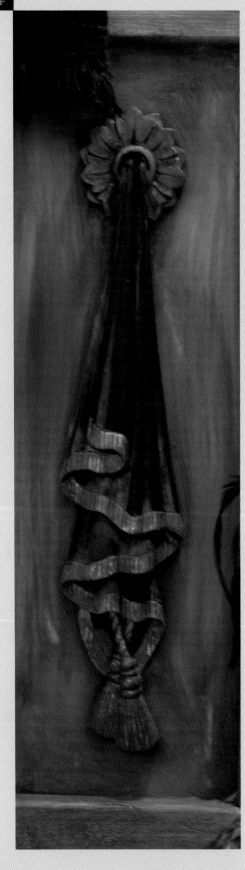

each door must be symmetrical if they are to frame a piece of furniture such as the bed.

• Step 3: Map out and measure the placement of the pine lattice strips that will frame and divide the decorative sections as described in Step 2.

• Step 4: Using a handsaw, cut the pine lattice strips and secure to the door with construction adhesive. One strip must be placed horizontally across each door along the top and bottom edges of where the side tables will be positioned. These strips will act as the back support for the side tables, so they must be attached very securely.

• Step 5: Measure and cut the flat wallpaper border to fit in the sections across the tops of the doors. Repeat with the embossed wallpaper border to fit in the sections across the tops of the side tables.

• Step 6: Begin distressing the lengths of flat wallpaper border by first wadding them up and getting them slightly damp under a faucet. Make certain you do not saturate the paper as it will begin to tear where it has been creased.

• Step 7: Carefully open up each length of distressed border and smooth it out to the best of your ability. They will have some wrinkles and tiny tears along the creases. This is the desired effect.

• Step 8: Using a damp sponge and metallic gold craft paint, lightly go over surface of each length of distressed border. If too much paint is applied, wipe off and start over until the desired "aging" effect is achieved. Let dry.

• Step 9: Using a paintbrush and wallpaper paste, apply a single length of distressed border to the sections across the tops of the doors. Let dry.

- Step 10: Apply a single length of embossed border to the sections across the tops of the side tables. Let dry.

- Step 11: Adhere the relief plaques in position with construction adhesive. Let dry.

- Step 12: Adhere the mirrored tiles in position with mirror adhesive. Let dry.

- Step 13: Caulk around all of the edges between pine lattice strips, wallpaper borders, and relief plaques.

    Do not caulk around the mirrored tiles.

- Step 14: Using a paintbrush, cover all of the wood surfaces, relief plaques, and lengths of embossed wallpaper border with gold flat latex paint. Let dry.

- Step 15: To simulate wood grain, lightly drag the paintbrush over the gold-painted surfaces with taupe flat latex paint. Let dry.

- Step 16: Using an electric screwdriver and wood screws, attach the doors to the wall.

- Step 17: Using a skillsaw, cut the dining table in half.

- Step 18: Position each table half into the pine lattice grooves on each backdrop.

- Step 19: Using the electric screwdriver and wood screws, attach the side tables to the backdrops.

- Step 20: Secure one decorative sconce to the front of each side table with wood screws or construction adhesive.

LAMP SHADES

Don't be intimidated by second-hand lamps with no shades. Before making your purchase, plug them in to make certain the electrical components are in good working order. Once you are satisfied that the lamp works, set out to find the perfect shade.

Department stores and home centers are generally rich sources for lamp shades of all sizes, styles, and colors. Take your thrift-store lamp with you and try different shades on it. You will be amazed at how the look of the lamp will change with each lamp shade you try.

I purchased these pheasant feather and tapestry shades for $19 each and placed them on $5 lamps.

I paid $30 for this antique lamp with beaded shade at a thrift store. At first I thought it was overpriced, but when I considered its true value, the price seemed reasonable. Realistically, I would have paid three times the amount had I purchased it at a retail antique specialty store.

This floor lamp was $10 at a discount outlet. It was dirty and had a lot of metal corrosion built-up on it, but nothing a little calcium, lime, and rust remover wouldn't eliminate. The lamp shade I chose had wonderful pattern and texture and was embellished with cut crystal and bead dangles.

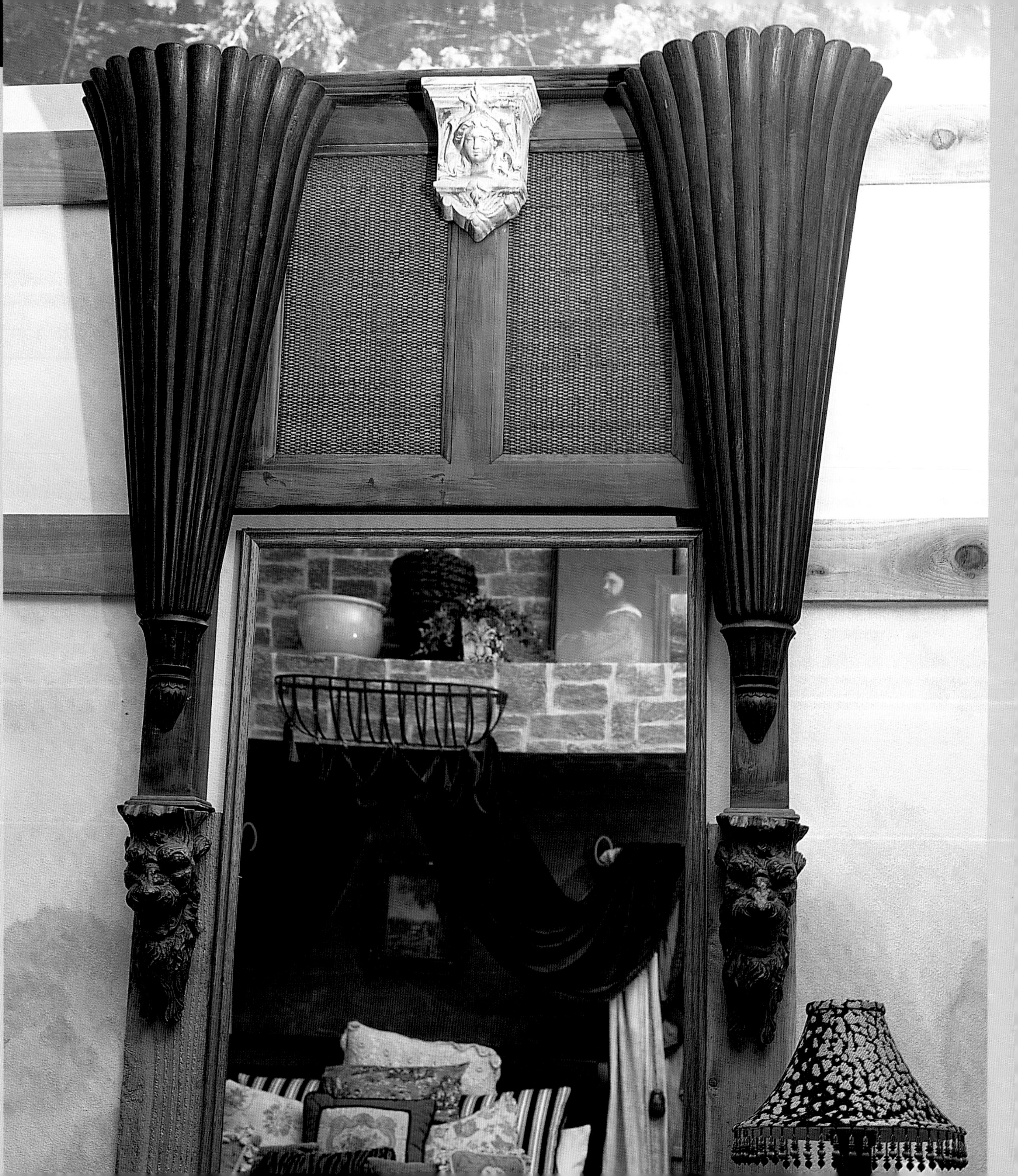

HEADBOARD & MIRROR WALL ART

After hanging this wardrobe mirror, it was apparent that the result was too plain! The mere height of the ceiling required something more. A search through the garage, looking for that perfect "something" to fill the empty void over the mirror, ended when I happened upon this $7 twin-sized headboard. Adding a large sconce at each side created the grandiose look this particular space needed.

MATERIALS

- Twin-sized headboard
- Wardrobe mirror
- Electric drill & drill bits
- Drywall anchors
- Cedar fencing:
  1" x 6" x 8', 3 lengths
- Wood screws
- Construction adhesive
- 2 Decorative sconces
- Resin wall bracket
- 2 Drapery corbels
- Paintbrush: 2" wide
- Flat latex paint: amber

WHAT TO DO

- Step 1: Acquire a twin-sized headboard that will fit over a wardrobe mirror and still clear the height of the ceiling.

- Step 2: Using an electric drill, install the headboard with drywall anchors.

- Step 3: Install the mirror with drywall anchors. The placement of the mirror should be as close to the bottom of the headboard as possible to create the illusion that the headboard is part of the framing around the mirror. The legs on the headboard will extend down both sides of the mirror for approximately 18".

- Step 4: Frame the sides and bottom of the mirror with lengths of cedar fencing. See "Cedar-fencing Woodwork" on pages 100–101.

- Step 5: Secure one decorative sconce to each side of the headboard with wood screws or construction adhesive. Adhere the resin wall bracket to the top center of the headboard and one drapery corbel to each side of the mirror where the legs on the headboard meet the cedar fencing.

- Step 6: Using a paintbrush, lightly drag amber latex paint over headboard and mirror frame.

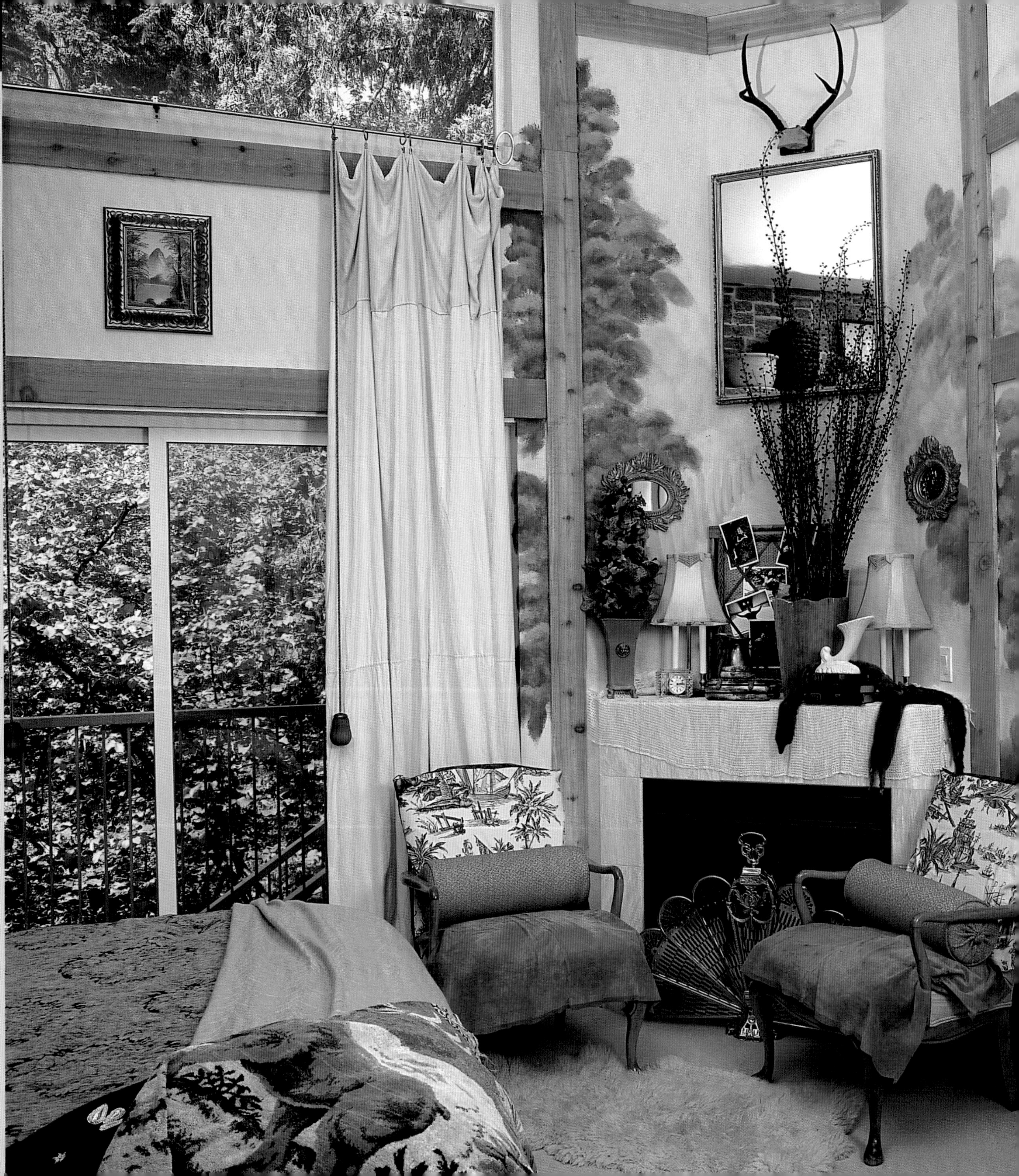

CEDAR-FENCING WOODWORK

I wanted the look of a French manor house in the master bedroom. I looked through books and magazines and the rooms I liked the most all had one feature in common: exposed woodwork and beams.

After I examined the configuration of my doors, windows, and wall decorations, I mapped out a plan as to where I would place the planks of cedar fencing. Then, the cedar was measured and cut to fit. Beginning with the horizontal planks, I installed the cedar with finishing nails. You will need to measure your doors and windows to determine the best positioning for your room to achieve the most realistic structural effect.

Keep in mind that before cutting the cedar fencing, it is imperative that it be completely dry. If wood is damp or "green," it will shrink, leaving unwanted gaps between joints. It is a good idea to bring the wood indoors and let it dry out for a couple of days before beginning your project.

If you want to achieve a weathered finish, a wash of light gray craft paint can be applied with a paintbrush. Apply the wash by using long brush strokes.

MURALS

Murals can enhance any wall regardless of the ceiling height or room size. The bedrooms in this house all have a ceiling height of 12'. The walls in the master suite begged for the royal treatment—something that would make them stand apart, but not steal the show. I had already decided that I wanted to enhance the French manor feel with murals, but I waited until all the cedar woodwork and wall decorations were in place before I started painting them.

For this layering technique, a car wash sponge, a 3"-wide paintbrush, and paints were the only things that I used.

The colors were chosen to complement and not compete with the color scheme. Rich golds, olive greens, soft browns, and grays were the foundation colors for the soft pastural scene that unifies the space and brings the white walls to life.

Our bedroom quickly became the family retreat. Everyone comes in to "hang out" and no one ever wants to leave!

MATERIALS

- Flat latex paints: amber, brown, olive green, off-white, taupe

- Car wash sponge

- Paintbrush: 3"-wide

- Craft paints: light gray, light green

WHAT TO DO

- Step 1: Mix amber and off-white flat latex paints to a warm gold shade. Using a large sponge, apply small amounts of this paint mixture to the top of your wall where the sky to your mural will begin. Make certain to allow portions of the wall to show through to simulate clouds. Use a "washing" motion and blend the paint to a soft, muted tone. Use this technique, working approximately half way down the wall. Fade to an almost white tone near the top of where your treetops will begin.

- Step 2: Using a paintbrush, begin to paint the treetop foliage with brown flat latex paint. In a "dabbing" motion, make small random rounded areas

Close-up of closet door mural. See page 106.

that will be the foundations for the remaining layers of foliage.

• Step 3: While the brown paint is still slightly wet, repeat Step 2 with olive green flat latex paint. In addition to layering over the brown areas of foliage, add some new ones with olive green.

• Step 4: Repeat Step 2 with light green craft paint.

• Step 5: Lightly dab over the tops of your foliage sections with the amber/off-white mixture to simulate sunlight meeting the leaves.

• Step 6: To paint the trees in the background, use the same technique with taupe flat latex paint and light gray craft paint. Mute the trees by adding off-white flat latex paint to all of the colors used in painting the trees in the background. Fade and layer the edges of the background foliage by gently wiping with a dry sponge. Use the same diluting and layering techniques for all additional background foliage.

MANTEL DISPLAY

There are many items that can be used as a mantel drape. Here I have used a prayer shawl.
I accented the shawl with fox furs for sentimental value. My grandfather was a silver-fox farmer and
I had always hoped to inherit a silver-fox fur. Unfortunately, they deteriorated over the years and had
to be disposed of. When I came across these at a local thrift store I knew I had to purchase them.
I added lighting to the mantel in the form of two small lamps, a collage of favorite family photos, and
some treasured knickknacks. I used vintage books to elevate some of the more interesting pieces.

CAFÉ DRAPES

There is no longer any reason for anyone to live in a "fish bowl" because they can't afford window coverings. One medium-weight 9' x 12' canvas drop cloth costs approximately $19 and is the best-kept secret at the hardware store! They can be dyed with fabric dyes, cut up, and sewn—even hot-glued. They can be embellished or left alone. They can be machine-washed and -dried, left wrinkled, or pressed. And, because of their versatility, you can have drop-cloth drapes in every room of your house and not have any two rooms ever look the same.

In the master bedroom, I purchased two drop cloths and hung them from the 9' side. I cut a thrift-store silk curtain in half and sewed one half to the 9' end of each drop cloth. I secured the top of the drapes with café curtain clips and strung them onto the rod. The edge is finished when purchased so there is no need to seam them. Instead of hemming the bottom, I left the excess to puddle on the floor for a more luxurious look.

DESK-TOP DISPLAYS

Once in a blue moon you're lucky enough to find something at a thrift store or flea market that you don't have to bring home and overhaul. Such is the case with this desk and chair.

If your display items all share something in common, it makes for a more interesting still life. You can also combine several items for an unusually stimulating presentation of common or ordinary objects. For my desk-top display, I chose color, theme, and shape. All the colors are either muted or neutral to bring unusual texture and depth to the desk top—without competing with the wall-mural backdrop. The theme is French manor. As your eye moves across the desk, the repeated conical shapes also bring continuity. The Eiffel Tower metal sculpture is a picture frame without the glass arch insets for photos. The metal garden topiary frame has good enough form to stand alone as architectural. Stacked wooden boxes and vintage French novels provide elevation for various pieces and add to the entire motif.

I have added light to the grouping with a wicker lamp. The color of the lamp base complements the colors of the surrounding objects. Finally, a mirror was hung on the wall above the desk to reflect the beautiful desk-top display of thrift-store treasures.

The desk shown in the photo above was used as a bedside table in our Utah home. I dressed-up the desk top, but left an ample amount of space so the desk could be functional.

FABRIC & FRINGE SIDE CHAIR

How many different ways can you "dress" a chair? I think that question will remain unanswered as long as there are glue guns and enough imagination to power them. It just keeps getting easier for me to spot an upholstery candidate hanging on a clothes rack at the thrift store!

This chair was covered with fabric remnants that included a brown velvet skirt and recycled fringe from thrift-store curtains. I further enhanced the look by draping a 5¢ lace table runner over the chair back and a $3 hand-crocheted satin-ribbon shawl over the edge. None of these fabrics are the same, yet they all work together beautifully because they are in the same color family.

MATERIALS

- Fabric remnants
- Old chair
- Hot-glue gun & glue sticks
- Scissors
- Recycled fringe

WHAT TO DO

- Step 1: Lay the desired fabric remnants over the area of the chair to be covered. Make certain to leave two to three inches of allowance on all sides.

  If using a remnant of clothing, remove collars, hems, sleeves, waistbands, pockets, zippers, and other closure mechanisms. If using a drapery, remove pleats and seams.

- Step 2: Beginning at the edge of the existing upholstery, secure the fabric to the side of the chair with hot glue. Let dry. Trim away excess fabric along glued and existing seams.

- Step 3: Pulling the opposite side of the fabric, stretch the fabric across the area to be covered until no wrinkling or puckering is visible. Apply hot glue to the edge and secure fabric. Repeat for the remaining two sides, then trim away excess fabric at each of the glued seams.

- Step 4: Repeat process on remaining parts of the chair to be covered.

- Step 5: Hot-glue recycled fringe over all glued and trimmed seams.

TIFFANY-STYLE CANDLEHOLDER

Second-hand stores and flea markets are usually overflowing with great lamps. Hanging lamps that are outdated and are oversized make spectacular table centerpieces. Remove all of the electrical components and turn the lamp upside down. You can fill them with candles, flowers, fruit, a large tossed green salad—even ice and chilled bottles of your favorite beverage.

I found this Tiffany-style lamp for $10. I brought it home, removed the lighting elements, and filled it with glass pebbles from the dollar store. I mixed some seashells in with the glass pebbles, then set a candle in the middle.

When lit, the candlelight not only makes the lamp bowl glow beautifully, it is reflected in the glass pebbles as well.

The space between the master bedroom and bath flows together, so it needed visual harmony. Warming the sterile space had its challenges, especially since the bedroom was so rich and intimate. I decided to carry the golds and silvers into the bathroom and warm it with soft browns and touches of black. Everything I did was aimed at breaking up all the right angles and redirecting the eye.

PLANT RACK TOWEL SHELF

This wonderfully rusted metal plant rack once lived in my yard. I relocated it to my bathroom and secured it to the wall by hanging it on two drywall-achored screws. You will need quite a bit of support to accommodate the weight of the glass and the towels.

I had glass cut for the shelves so they would be more functional for storage and display. The silver swag on the front was purchased at a discount store, then washed with brown craft paint to antique it. I attached it to the plant rack with floral wire.

SIDE TABLE LUXURIES

What's more inviting in the bath than a cache of bath-time luxuries within reach? If you don't have room for a permanent table somewhere close to the bathtub, this one could be the solution to such a dilemma. This table is made from a plant stand and serving platter. It places soaps, oils, towels, and candles at your fingertips so your bath can be more of a soaking, relaxing get-away.

The pictures on the tray table are collected gifts, thrift-store and discount-store purchases, or items used from other rooms in the house. This idea functions much like an end table next to your favorite chair. Now your bathtub can have the same draw. When bath time comes to an end, simply place the plant back on the stand and return the furnishing to its prior home.

SUN STONE TILE PLAQUES

Louis XIV of France chose the sun as his royal emblem, and thereafter became known as the "Sun King." He decorated his 17th century palace with an extravagance not seen since. The sunburst design is one of the few design elements from centuries past that is still seen in modern design. The warmth of these timeless images adds to the coziness of this master bath.

I purchased 32 of these sun plaques at the dollar

store. I thought perhaps I would install them on the backsplash in my kitchen, set right next to each other. Instead, I adhered one over the window treatment in the master bathroom and placed four, evenly spaced, across the front of our jetted tub.

They added so much, I decided to use more of these sun plaques elsewhere in my home. I have them in the hallway as part of a mural and in the formal living room centered over each curtain rod as shown in the photo on page 60.

LAYERED FRAMES

A great-looking frame is a great asset! The large black, gold-leafed frame was purchased exactly as you see it. It was part of several discontinued frames available at the craft store for 75% off the lowest clearance price. It serves as the highest point in the grouping over the jetted tub and as a second frame for the picture below it.

Instead of a wall, I'm using the window and the window ledge to support the eclectic collection of found objects.

FRAMED HANDMADE PAPER BOTANICAL

Dryer lint has an abundance of fibers. The colors are endless and the possibilities are limitless for the varied combinations you can dream up. Papermakers pay good money for fibers to add to their handmade papers, but you can use what you find in your dryer's lint trap.

The botanical is covered with a piece of used dryer sheet for a slightly transparent effect. Placed in a faux-silver-leafed thrift-store frame, you have a sophisticated-looking work of art that you can hang in any room of your home.

MATERIALS

- Dryer lint: 4 cups
- Large metal pan
- Water: 2 cups
- Metal spatula
- 2 Brown-paper grocery bags
- Heavy-duty, water-soluble wallpaper paste: 3 cups
- Cookie sheet
- Botanical
- Craft glue
- Used dryer sheet
- Metallic silver thread
- Faux-silver leafing & adhesive
- Frame

WHAT TO DO

- Step 1: To make the handmade paper, tear the dryer lint into small sections and place in a large metal pan. Add water and stir with a metal spatula.

- Step 2: Tear brown-paper grocery bags into small pieces and add to the mixture in the metal pan.

- Step 3: Add heavy-duty wallpaper paste to mixture and mix thoroughly.

- Step 4: Bring mixture to a boil, stirring constantly. Cook mixture until paper pieces turn to pulp.

- Step 5: Pour mixture onto cookie sheet. Bake in oven

at 300° until water evaporates and paper is dry. Let cool. Remove the rubbery paper from cookie sheet.

Do not overcook, as the paper will start to turn dark around the edges.

• Step 6: Position botanical on paper and adhere in place with craft glue. Let dry.

• Step 7: Cut a square from a used dryer sheet.

• Step 8: Cover the botanical with the square of dryer sheet and stitch around the edges with thread.

• Step 9: Apply silver-leafing adhesive to the frame and let dry until it is no longer tacky to the touch. Apply the faux-silver leafing ac-

cording to manufacturer's directions.

• Step 10: Back the handmade paper with a brown-paper grocery bag. Make certain to use the side without printing on it.

• Step 11: Mat the handmade paper botanical. Place into the prepared frame and secure.

BROKEN-POT RELIEF WORK

Have you ever broken a beautiful pot or planter that just pained you to have to throw away? Next time, don't fret. With the help of a little plaster of paris and concrete, you can have a beautiful new addition to a wall, fireplace mantel, backsplash, or bathtub. You can get plaster of paris in a container about the size of a half-gallon of milk or in a 25-pound bag. If you have multiple pieces from a large broken pot or planter, you may opt for the larger bag.

This simple architectural element is so easy to make. Using a small box as a form, you can create any size or shape you want. Painted after construction, it looks like the broken pot piece and the base were poured together to form the relief. With the magic of faux, you can choose any "stone" you wish, then paint the relief accordingly.

MATERIALS

- Small shallow box
- Waxed paper
- Latex gloves
- Plaster of paris
- 1 Bag concrete
- Disposable container
- Rubber spatula
- Broken pieces of pot or planter
- Wire brush
- Paintbrush
- Outdoor latex paint
- Matte acrylic spray sealer

WHAT TO DO

- Step 1: Completely line the box with waxed paper. Make certain to leave approximately a 3" overlap on all sides.

- Step 2: Wearing latex gloves, mix equal parts of plaster of paris and concrete in a disposable container. Add water until you have a creamy consistency.

- Step 3: Pour mixture into waxed-paper-lined box and smooth with flat-edged rubber spatula.

- Step 4: Place broken pot/planter piece into center of box and press into mixture. Adjust as needed.

- Step 5: Set in a warm place to speed drying time. Let dry.

- Step 6: Using the overlapped edges of waxed paper as handles and tipping the box, remove the formed relief.

- Step 7: Using a wire brush, wear down the surface area and the sides to the desired effect.

- Step 8: Using a paintbrush, apply the desired faux-stone finish with outdoor latex paint. Seal with matte acrylic spray sealer.

LINEN LAYERING

Quality linen never goes out of style. If you have an abundant supply in the linen closet, it's time to bring it out of hiding and into the spotlight. I didn't have many pieces of fine linen; but after a few concerted trips to the thrift store, I had all I needed for two bathrooms.

Large cloth napkins made from nicer quality fabrics can double as fingertip towels. Crocheted doilies in intricate shapes and patterns turn an ordinary towel into extra-ordinary. The mix-and-match rule is the only one observed here. I stayed with a soft neutral color scheme and played with different layering formations until I was happy with the end result.

To add a sense of whimsy to your ensemble, include something interesting such as a necklace, a small beaded purse, or other assorted objects. I found this picture stopwatch of a Venetian street scene at the thrift store for $11. It is nice to be able to visit Venice whenever bath time comes around.

TRADING PLACES

Most objects have a purpose, but there is much fun in using an object in an unconventional way. Such is the case with this English toast holder. I have transformed it into a bathroom necessity. It holds a single washcloth and a bar of my favorite french-milled soap!

VINTAGE CANDELABRA

Vintage chandeliers make wonderful hanging candelabras. If you don't want to have a fixture rewired or you don't have existing wiring where you want to hang it, simply place candles in it instead!

I found this rose chandelier at a flea market for $13. The gold-leafed and red-rose metal vine intertwined throughout the light fixture was $1 at the goodwill outlet. Both of the candelabra sleeves were missing, so I cut two 3" lengths from copper pipe with a hacksaw, placed them over the lighting elements, and set votive candles on top of them. Make certain to check the burning time of your candles.

CABINET-DOOR
SCULPTURE

A flat boring cabinet is not a problem, it's a blank canvas! By applying add-ons like these, you instantly give the appearance of a carving without going to great expense. Whenever you have the chance to buy more than one of these types of resin plaques, seize the opportunity. You never know when you will need them for repetitious decorating.

SUSPENDED PICTURE FRAME

Look again. The gold frame shown here is just that—an empty frame! I bought it at the goodwill outlet for $15 and purchased chain-by-the-foot at the home center. The frame is suspended in front of the large sheet mirror above the sinks in my bathroom. Because the frame is empty it is extremely lightweight, making it easy to hang. The elegance it brings into this space is substantial.

SEASHELL
TOWEL HOLDERS

A special person in my life gave me these shells and I have used them for many different purposes throughout my home at one time or another. They are very beautiful in color and form and the fact that their function has so many variables makes them even more wonderful! I am currently using them as holders for my bathroom hand towels.

GUEST
QUARTERS

VINTAGE BED

An iron bed is an asset anywhere in your home or yard. Before I found this bed at the thrift store for $30, our daughter had a traditional bed in her room. I love the color and the natural wear-and-tear the vintage bed has undergone through many years of use. The medallions on the head- and footboards and the metal caning make it a perfectly "French" anchor for the rest of the bedroom.

This bed works great with the selection of second-hand linens that was used because it provides the visual contrast necessary to bring interest into the space. I had the color scheme and the overall theme of this room present in my mind everytime I went on a shopping spree. Luckily I was able to collect bags full of compatible linens. Sorting through and choosing our favorites became the most difficult part of the project. Layering the linens on the bed allowed us to use more than we thought we could and gave us unlimited ways of using various textures, patterns, and colors.

WINDOW-FRAME MIRROR

Old windows make great mirrors. Simply add mirror to an empty window frame or replace the window glass with mirror. This window frame was distressed with the same paint and technique as the "Découpage Desk" on pages 134–135. It adds another layer of windows and light.

VINTAGE PLATE WALL ART

Vintage plates make great wall art! In fact, any great-looking dinnerware makes for whimsical decorating accents.

All the plates and bowls on the walls or on display in this bedroom were collected from thrift stores on several different shopping trips. This is also a great way to use the few pieces of your grandmother's china that you treasure, but weren't really certain how to display.

It will serve you well to start gathering a collection of plates, bowls, and saucers that can be "reincarnated" into decorative conversation pieces. An eclectic collection of anything brings character and style.

ROSE DRAPERY ACCENTS

The rings holding the curtains on the rod are miniature wired paper-rose garlands that I purchased at the local craft store. The small floral bouquets are wired on the ends to "anchor" the presentation. The white lace panel in the center softens the sliding glass door without restricting the light.

ACRYLIC-CAULK VINES

This inexpensive idea was the result of wanting to add to the visually flat surface on the closet doors. I wanted the effect to look as if the vines were carved into the door. One $1.29 tube of caulk did both closet doors and the bathroom door.

MATERIALS

- Paintable acrylic latex caulk
- Caulking gun
- Foam brush: 2"-wide
- Flat latex paint: desired color

WHAT TO DO

• Step 1: Snip the top off the tube of caulk. Make certain to keep the opening small; the larger the hole, the larger the vine. Load into a caulking gun.

• Step 2: Lightly map out your vine design with a pencil. Using medium pressure, place the end of the tube of caulk onto the surface and begin squeezing caulk over the design. Let dry.

If too much caulk comes out, wipe away excess with a very damp rag.

• Step 3: To make the leaves, squeeze a small dot of caulk next to the vine. Slightly pulling away from the vine, drag the dot into a leaf shape. Using a wet finger, gently press each leaf to slightly flatten and shape. Let dry.

• Step 4: Using a foam brush, paint all of the vines and leaves in the same shade of flat latex paint as the door or wall. Let dry.

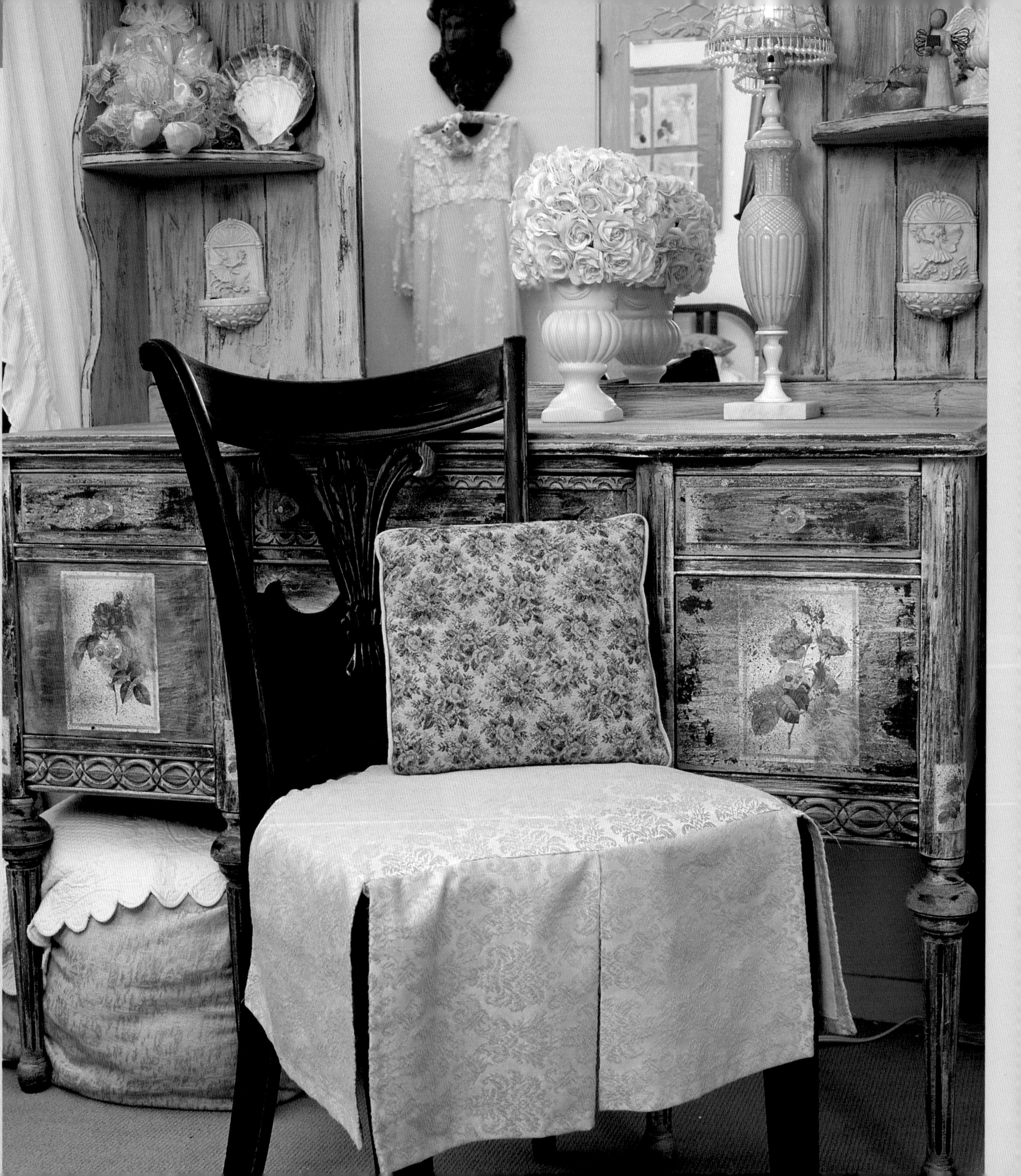

DÉCOUPAGE DESK

Right from the start this piece was one of those love-at-first-sight projects. I bought it at the goodwill outlet for $30. It was partially stripped which revealed that the wood on the drawers was not the same as the wood on the rest of the desk. With new handles, découpaged rose note cards, and some paint, this ugly duckling desk quickly turned fabulous!

MATERIALS

- Desk
- Paintbrush: 3"-wide
- Flat latex paint: white
- Rose note cards
- Heavy-duty, water-soluble wallpaper paste
- Craft paint: pink
- Spray paint: brown satin
- Stripper
- 60-grit sandpaper
- Satin acrylic sealer

WHAT TO DO

- Step 1: Remove all handles and hardware.

- Step 2: If desk is painted or stained, you may opt to strip some of the original layer in order to allow portions of the raw wood to show through. Using a paintbrush, lightly streak white flat latex paint over the entire desk in a dragging motion. Let dry.

- Step 3: Apply the rose note cards as desired on the desk with wallpaper paste. Let dry.

- Step 4: Repeat Step 2 along the edges of the desk with pink craft paint.

- Step 5: Using very little pressure, spray the brown satin paint in a spattering pattern over the entire desk.

Make certain to practice on a piece of newspaper to determine how much pressure is required.

- Step 6: Lightly brush stripper over selected areas. Let stripper bubble, then let dry. Lightly sand over areas.

- Step 7: Seal with multiple coats of satin acrylic sealer. Let dry between each coat.

- Step 8: Replace handles and hardware.

BLACK VENETIAN DESK CHAIR

This technique can be used on any piece of furniture with any color combination. The only helpful hint to remember is to have the trim color be enough of a contrast that it sets off the details you want accented.

MATERIALS

- Wooden chair

- Sandpapers:
  60-grit, 100-grit

- Paintbrush: 3"-wide

- Flat latex paint: black

- Foam brush: 1"-wide

- Craft paint:
  metallic Venetian gold

WHAT TO DO

- Step 1: Using 100-grit sandpaper, lightly sand wood areas of chair.

- Step 2: Using a paintbrush, paint chair with black latex paint. Let dry.

- Step 3: Using a foam brush, paint the edges of the chair and any raised

details with metallic Venetian-gold craft paint. Let dry.

- Step 4: Using 60-grit sandpaper, sand off paint layers allowing portions of the raw wood to show through.

FRAMED VINTAGE GLOVES

I could think of no one I knew with hands dainty enough to fit into the vintage crocheted gloves I found at the thrift store for $2. In spite of their lack of functionality, I had to have them. It's been fun imagining who might have worn them and what small hands they must have held. I am certain the hands that occupied them never used a power tool, painted a house, or gardened in the dirt with wild abandon. No matter what, they would now be mine—not to wear, but to frame and memorialize.

Brown packing paper was used as the backdrop for these vintage pieces, then double-sided tape was used to adhere them in place on the brown paper. A simple wooden frame, painted white, was chosen to finish off the look of the consummate, absolute, girly girl.

MEMO-BOARD COLLAGE

This memo board is hanging on a hollow-core door covered in the same French limestone wall-paper as shown in the formal living room on page 60. Plant hooks are installed at each side with tab-topped gauze drapery panels hanging from them. The actual memo board was purchased at the goodwill outlet for $2.99. We use it as a display for some of our favorite vintage note cards. Family photos are also fun to collage into this type of memo board.

CANDLELIER

A find at $3, this pale pink chandelier looked just like this at a tag sale. I carted it from Utah and stashed it away. When I first showed it to my daughter Chelsea, she loved it.

I put two votive candles on the light fixture and turned it into a "candlelier." I found the distressed grate at my local craft store for $10 and mounted the fixture on it. It gives a lot of character to the otherwise blank side of the closet armoire.

This same technique could be used with a vintage birdcage. Instead of placing votive candles, fill the cage with silk flowers and/or a bird statuette. A birdcage could be mounted to the distressed grate just as the candlelier was.

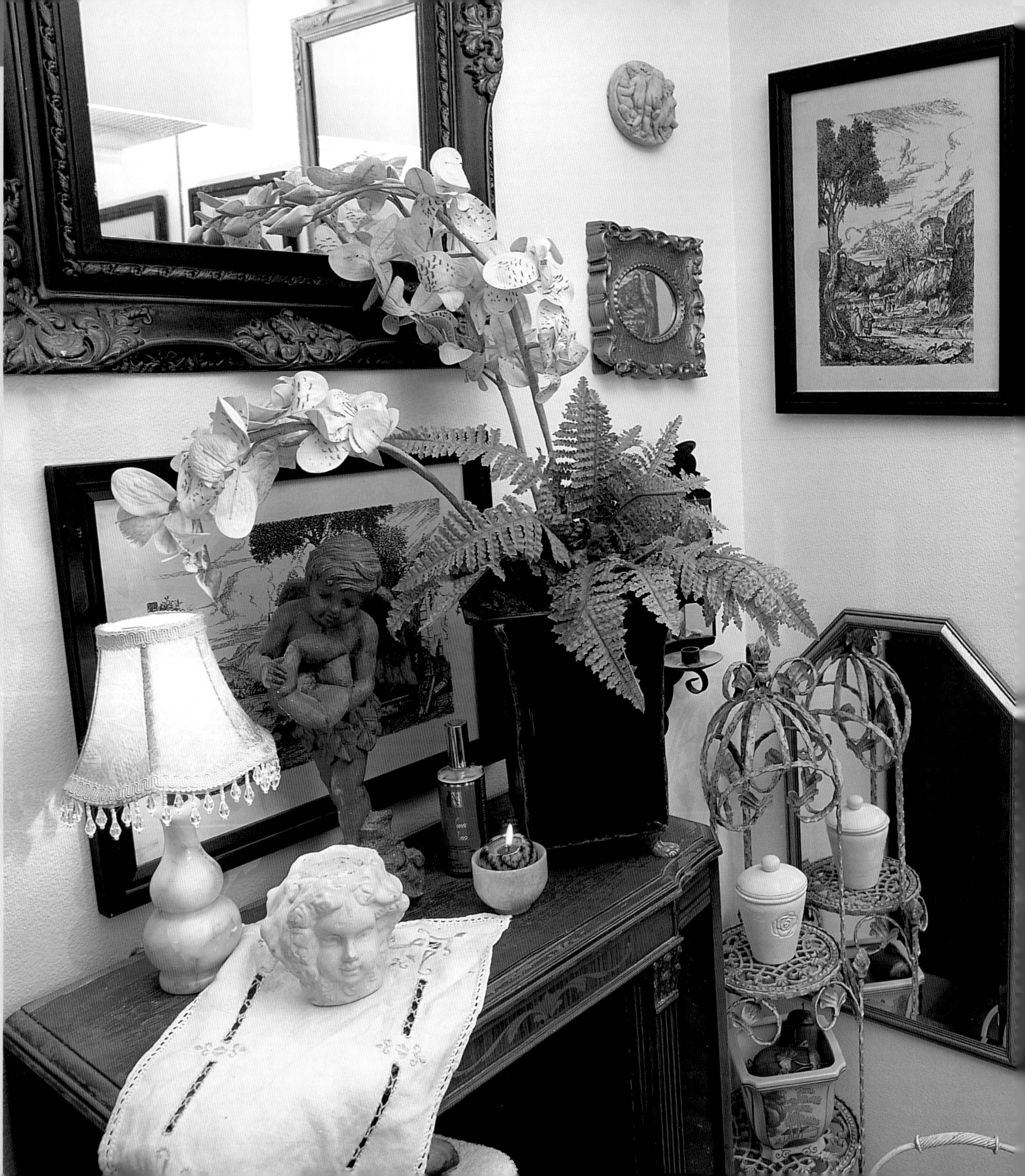

WALL-TO-WALL FRAMES

If you have a small guest bath, you will reap great rewards from wallscaping with whatever makes you happy. The only rule you need to be concerned about is establishing a common theme.

In one of the very few rooms left in my house with plain white walls, I chose to use a neutral color scheme of black-and-white, accented with taupes and golds. This was a choice dictated out of necessity. The vanity and countertop would have to remain, so that determined my starting point.

I had collected a large assortment of mirrors on all my junking adventures and they were a must

to visually enlarge the space. The set of black-and-gold lithographs were another must for my wallscape, purchased at the thrift store for $14.99. I wanted to keep them all together for impact.

The secret to wallscaping is to remember that any exposed wall, from floor to ceiling, should be considered fair game in French country decorating. Oftentimes, the French had very small country homes that they would fill wall-to-wall with objets d'art to impress guests that had been invited for a weekend stay. Filling the room full of such treasures and collections gives the room an important look and helps the guest feel welcome.

TOWEL CHEST

This antique radio cabinet is enjoying a new life as storage space in our guest bath. Its open shelves create ample space for storing hand towels, accessories, and magazines.

I insist on having a place for magazines in the bathroom since that is seemingly the only time I get to soak, relax, and look through them.

I use outdoor statuary in all of my bathrooms for conversational guest soap holders. They also provide countertop plat-forming so I can layer other beautiful things beneath them. Statues like this angel are perfect because of their height and dimension.

The black wire basket is holding an assortment of guest hand towels. Since the basket has a lid, it makes the towels seem like the bathroom guest is opening a treasure to get to them. The little boy garden sculpture provides a perfect presentation for the bars of French-milled soap. Layering a mirror against the existing wall-mounted one adds visual interest.

LE JARDIN

WALL ART

The front of the house was a good place to provide something of interest on the otherwise very long plain wall connecting the house and the garage.

These unique faux raised-copper panels that were used at our daughter's wedding were the right choice. Made from metal louvered doors, accented with embossed-wallpaper border, ceiling medallions, and paint, we spaced the panels at equal intervals across the front of the house to simulate a French villa veranda. Because these panels are displayed outside, several coats of polyurethane sealer is highly recommended.

GARDEN DRESSER

I love using old dressers and vanities as potting benches. This is a great way to use furniture that is distressed or weathered past the point for indoor usage. Any cupboard space can be used to store out-of-service pots and potting tools.

FIREPLACE
FOUNTAIN

This fountain is the jewel of the front yard. The brass planter box underneath it is an old fireplace apron turned into a planter. The black fence sections flanking the fountain are fireplace screens.

TRAY-TABLE PEDESTAL

Any outside dining area benefits from a casual service of food to encourage leisure nibbling. Serving assorted breads, fruits, and cheeses is perfect on any occasion. It's so French!

This table is made from a brass tray set on top of a plaster pedestal. The chairs were hand-distressed by randomly dragging a rag saturated with paint thinner over the black paint.

Similar to the wooden tray table in the master bath, this applies the same principles of pairing salvaged items to make functional furniture. If you require a tabletop that is completely flat, a round piece of glass is recommended.

MATERIALS

- Brass tray
- Spray paint: white
- 100-grit sandpaper
- Plaster pedestal
- Construction adhesive

WHAT TO DO

- Step 1: Spray the brass tray with white spray paint.
- Step 2: Lightly sand the surface of the brass tray to expose the glow of the brass in select areas.
- Step 3: Adhere the brass tray to the top of the pedestal with construction adhesive. Let dry.

VERANDA BED

This twin-size bed fits into this snug alcove like it was a custom fit. The antique bed came from the goodwill outlet and was $60. It is one of those pieces that had already aged and yellowed to a warm and welcoming patina. I didn't do anything with it except put it together.

The thrift-store mattress cost $15 and the box spring cost $10. I wrapped them both in a heavy-plastic drop cloth and closed the package with duct tape. This will aid greatly in keeping the bugs and the moisture from coming into direct contact with the mattress/box-spring fabrics.

Make certain to cover the plastic-wrapped mattress/box spring with a good quality mattress pad, followed by any bed linens you wish to use. To complete this ensemble, randomly scatter accent pillows on the bed.

TOPIARY SCREEN

Hollow-core doors and ¹/₈" hardboard come together to create this serene backdrop to the veranda. Each panel has been secured to one hollow-core door, then the doors were hinged together, allowing them to stand independently.

The tops of the panels were shaped with a jigsaw and wooden ornaments were added. The height of the topiary panels surpass the height of the doors, but the doors are heavy enough to support the excess.

Hand-painting your own design on the fronts is rewarding, but a collage of botanical prints or black-and-white family photos can be découpaged onto each panel. Also, wallpaper can be adhered to each panel with heavy-duty wallpaper paste.

MOSS-COVERED PEDESTAL

You can easily cultivate, grow, and maintain live moss on your pots all year-round—ssshhh! don't tell Mother Nature.

Using a 2"-wide paintbrush, apply live cultured yogurt to the areas on the surface of the pot you want to grow moss. Then, gently wrap the entire pot with damp paper towels. Place the pot in a dark place. You will want the paper towels to stay damp, so spray them regularly with a spray bottle filled with water. This will begin to cultivate the live cultures in the yogurt and moss will begin to grow. Once your pot is covered with a soft-green haze, remove the paper towels and move the pot into indirect sunlight. On a weekly basis, spray the pot with beer as the hops will keep the moss rich and green.

METRIC CONVERSIONS

INCHES TO MILLIMETRES AND CENTIMETRES

MM-Millimetres   CM-Centimetres

INCHES	MM	CM	INCHES	CM	INCHES	CM
1/8	3	0.9	9	22.9	30	76.2
1/4	6	0.6	10	25.4	31	78.7
3/8	10	1.0	11	27.9	32	81.3
1/2	13	1.3	12	30.5	33	83.8
5/8	16	1.6	13	33.0	34	86.4
3/4	19	1.9	14	35.6	35	88.9
7/8	22	2.2	15	38.1	36	91.4
1	25	2.5	16	40.6	37	94.0
1 1/4	32	3.2	17	43.2	38	96.5
1 1/2	38	3.8	18	45.7	39	99.1
1 3/4	44	4.4	19	48.3	40	101.6
2	51	5.1	20	50.8	41	104.1
2 1/2	64	6.4	21	53.3	42	106.7
3	76	7.6	22	55.9	43	109.2
3 1/2	89	8.9	23	58.4	44	111.8
4	102	10.2	24	61.0	45	114.3
4 1/2	114	11.4	25	63.5	46	116.8
5	127	12.7	26	66.0	47	119.4
6	152	15.2	27	68.6	48	121.9
7	178	17.8	28	71.1	49	124.5
8	203	20.3	29	73.7	50	127.0

YARDS TO METRES

YARDS	METRES	YARDS	METRES	YARDS	METRES	YARDS	METRES	YARDS	METRES
1/8	0.11	2 1/8	1.94	4 1/8	3.77	6 1/8	5.60	8 1/8	7.43
1/4	0.23	2 1/4	2.06	4 1/4	3.89	6 1/4	5.72	8 1/4	7.54
3/8	0.34	2 3/8	2.17	4 3/8	4.00	6 3/8	5.83	8 3/8	7.66
1/2	0.46	2 1/2	2.29	4 1/2	4.11	6 1/2	5.94	8 1/2	7.77
5/8	0.57	2 5/8	2.40	4 5/8	4.23	6 5/8	6.06	8 5/8	7.89
3/4	0.69	2 3/4	2.51	4 3/4	4.34	6 3/4	6.17	8 3/4	8.00
7/8	0.80	2 7/8	2.63	4 7/8	4.46	6 7/8	6.29	8 7/8	8.12
1	0.91	3	2.74	5	4.57	7	6.40	9	8.23
1 1/8	1.03	3 1/8	2.86	5 1/8	4.69	7 1/8	6.52	9 1/8	8.34
1 1/4	1.14	3 1/4	2.97	5 1/4	4.80	7 1/4	6.63	9 1/4	8.46
1 3/8	1.26	3 3/8	3.09	5 3/8	4.91	7 3/8	6.74	9 3/8	8.57
1 1/2	1.37	3 1/2	3.20	5 1/2	5.03	7 1/2	6.86	9 1/2	8.69
1 5/8	1.49	3 5/8	3.31	5 5/8	5.14	7 5/8	6.97	9 5/8	8.80
1 3/4	1.60	3 3/4	3.43	5 3/4	5.26	7 3/4	7.09	9 3/4	8.92
1 7/8	1.71	3 7/8	3.54	5 7/8	5.37	7 7/8	7.20	9 7/8	9.03
2	1.83	4	3.66	6	5.49	8	7.32	10	9.14

INDEX

Acrylic-caulk Vines 132–133
Antique Mirror 83
Before, During & After ... 16–19
Before You Begin 13
Black Venetian
    Desk Chair 136
Broken-pot
    Relief Work............. 118–119
Buffet Display 74–75
Cabinet-door Sculpture 123
Cabinet-top
    Hutch Display 3, 38–39
Café Drapes 105
Candlelier.......................... 139
Cedar-fencing
    Woodwork 100–101
Cloison Display 84–85
Copper Cabinets 22–25
Countertop Displays 34–35
Découpage Desk 134–135
Desk-top Displays 106–107
Dining Room & Entry 72–87
Distressed Folding
    Screen 54–57
Entryway Ledge
    Displays 86–87
Fabric & Fringe
    Side Chair 108–109
Fascia Carvings 40
Faux Hammered-pewter
    Buffet 76–78
Faux-slate Wallpaper 30–32
Faux-stone Add-ons &
    Brackets 51
Fireplace Fountain 149
Fireplace Hood 48–50

Flower-basket
    Chandelier 2, 42–43
Flower Rack &
    Bedspread Canopy 90–91
Formal Living Room . 1, 46–71
Framed Handmade-
    paper Botanical....... 116–117
Framed Vintage Gloves 137
French Limestone
    Wallpaper 60–61
Fringed Drop-cloth
    Drapery...................... 58–59
From Junk to Objets d'Art ... 8–9
Garden Dresser................ 148
Guest Quarters 126–143
Half-table Side Tables &
    Backdrops 92–95
Headboard &
    Footboard Sofa 66–69
Headboard & Mirror
    Wall Art 98–99
Kitchen & Bistro 2, 20–45
Lamp Shades 96–97
Layered Frames 115
Le Jardin 144–154
Library Display 52–53
Linen Layering 120–121
Mantel Display 104
Marbled Table 80–82
Master Suite 88–125
Memo-board Collage 138
Metric Conversions 155
Moss-covered Pedestal 154
Murals 102–103
Nutty Topiaries 36–37
Pillow Panache 65

Plant Rack
    Towel Shelf 112–113
Range Hood Plaques 26–27
Recessed Display 33
Rose Drapery Accents 131
Seashell Towel Holders 125
Shawl Swag Curtain........44–45
Shower-curtain-covered
    Chairs 62–64
Side Table Luxuries .. 112–113
Silverware Handles &
    Drawer Pulls 28–29
Sun Stone
    Tile Plaques 114–115
Suspended Picture
    Frame 124
Swag-draped Wall Mirror 79
Tabletop Displays 70–71
Textured Soffit Tile 41
The Day's Findings
    Must Be Stored 12
The Search Begins 10–11
Tiffany-style Candleholder .. 110
Topiary Screen.......... 152–153
Towel Chest..................... 142
Trading Places 120–121
Tray-table Pedestal ... 150–151
Veranda Bed 152–153
Vintage Bed 128–129
Vintage Candelabra 122
Vintage Plate Wall Art 131
Wall Art 146–147
Wall-to-wall Frames ... 140–141
Welcome To Our
    Oregon Home 14–15
Window-frame Mirror 130